**IS
THERE
REALLY
ONLY
<u>ONE</u>
WAY?**

IS
THERE
REALLY
ONLY
ONE
WAY?

IS
THERE
REALLY
ONLY
<u>ONE</u>
WAY?

Dick Hillis

Man's future is forever...
...but where?

VISION HOUSE PUBLISHERS
Santa Ana, California 92705

IS THERE REALLY ONLY ONE WAY?
Copyright © 1974 Vision House Publishers
Santa Ana, California 92705
ISBN 0-88449-005-X Paperback
Library of Congress Catalogue Number 74-75877

Acknowledgments:

THE SUPREME TASK OF THE CHURCH, by Dr. J. T.
Seamands, copyright 1964 by the author, by permission of
William B. Eerdmans Publishing Company, Grand Rapids,
Michigan

NEW AMERICAN STANDARD BIBLE, and NEW
TESTAMENT, 1960, 1962, 1963, 1968, 1971, the Lockman
Foundation; used by permission.

Printed In The United States of America

Dedicated
to
all who care
or
want to care
about
the spiritual condition
of
their fellow men.

GUIDEPOSTS

Chapter   Page

PART I

1. SINCERELY YOURS...................................   3
2. THE LIGHT SWITCHED OFF....................   9
3. LADDER OF STRAW...............................   17
4. I GOT RELIGION   25
5. "I COULD HAVE TOUCHED GOD"............   33
6. WALK THROUGH A GRAVEYARD............   41
7. ONLY ONE WAY!....................................   51
8. IS GOD CRUEL?.....................................   59

PART II

9. SOME SINS ARE NICER THAN OTHERS...   69
10. WHO KILLED "CONCERN"?.....................   77
11. THAT HAND ON MY WALLET...................   87
12. MY ACHING KNEES!...............................   93
13. JUMP IN – OR COP OUT!......................... 103
14. "HOW DO I FIT IN?"................................ 111

PREFACE

There is an exciting movement today from casual Christianity to committed discipleship. Perhaps it is born of the desperate moment in which we live, or just an inevitable extension of the spiritual roots to reach deeper and sweeter waters. In any case, Dick Hillis's book will prove an invaluable aid toward Christian maturity.

Coming out of a background of intensive missionary labor, and acquainted with Oriental mysteries, he is well qualified to write about other "religions" and pagan cultures. His contrast with the truth of the Gospel comes out with moving clarity.

Even the headings of the fourteen chapters are laden with "reading appeal," and throughout the development of the book, Mr. Hillis maintains an attitude of honest inquiry. The conclusion is always arrived at with definitive logic. Christ is the Truth—His way, indeed the only way.

Dick writes with a colloquial freshness; the extensive use of Biblical support gives it a holy imperative.

I hope this book will point many to the cross in repentance and faith, and will spur Christ's church to new levels of witnessing activity while it is "yet day" for the "one way."

Billy Graham

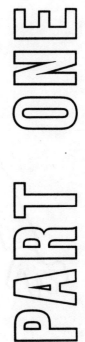

PART ONE

Man's Future is Forever,
... but WHERE?

CHAPTER 1

◆

SINCERELY YOURS

I have watched thousands of worshipers in the Orient bow before man-made gods. My first reaction was to silently ridicule. How stupid and naive can they be? I thought.

They hire a carpenter to nail the wooden "bones" together and a mason then fashions the muscles and flesh with wet mud. For a little higher price or bigger meal, he will form a female deity. When the mud is dry, a local artist adds brilliant colors to the drab mud god. Then under the watchful eye and practical guidance of a golden-robed priest, the idol, after being given an altar and incense burner, is dedicated as the all-sufficient village god.

But before I made a further judgment about their sanity, I decided to ask why they bowed before these idols. "Madam," I said, "for the last ten minutes you have been on your knees bowing before that deity. Would you please tell me why?"

"Sir," she replied, "my husband is out of work. My children are hungry. The landlord has threatened to throw us out. My burdens are heavy and I am asking for help."

"And you, Sir," I said, "I noticed you gave a

bushel of rice to the priest. Then as the temple bells began to ring the priest shook a box filled with bamboo sticks until one fell on the ground. Would you please tell me what all this means?"

"The bushel of rice," said the man, "is my offering to our god. The bamboo stick has an answer to prayer inscribed on it."

"And what was the priest praying for?" I asked.

"We have seven children. The youngest is two weeks old. Her mother is very sick. The midwife can't stop her bleeding. She has a fever and won't eat and I am afraid for my children and their mother's life."

The answer to why people bow before gods who have eyes and cannot see and ears and cannot hear, is simple. They have burdens they cannot carry and fears they cannot quiet. They have never met the One who said, "Come to Me, all who are weary and heavy laden, and I will give you rest" (Matthew 11:28ff).

Another question crossed my mind as I stood in the temple compound. Are these idol worshipers sincere in their beliefs? But then the question backfired as I thought about my own sincerity and the sincerity of the average Christian who attends an average morning church service. Are these more sincere than those who prostrate themselves before a mud god?

When I want a "study in sincerity" I watch worshipers in a heathen temple. Their faces are laced with worry and concern; one sees no nonsense or laughter and I am forced to conclude if sincerity could save, many of these people would be saved. The hard fact is that sincerity does not, cannot, save! It's possible to be absolutely sincere and at the same time, absolutely wrong.

One of the most sincere men in the New Testament was a Pharisee named Nicodemus. Most of the Pharisees, however, were anything but sincere. And Jesus reserved His harshest words of condemnation for the Pharisees' counterfeit piety calling them "whited sepulchres". But Nicodemus was of a different stripe. He carefully fulfilled every ritual of the strictest religious Jewish sect. He was a religious man and no one questioned his deep sincerity. Yet with all his sincerity he knew something was missing. His faithful religious practices did not quiet his guilty conscience, give him peace with God, or take away the fear of dying and standing before a holy God. Nicodemus was sincere but lost, and he sensed it. If sincerity were enough, this ultra-religious Pharisee would never have turned to Jesus.

Today, a man like Nicodemus would be considered an ideal member of many churches—even a candidate for deacon or elder. After all, wasn't he a highly respected member of the Sanhedrin, brilliantly educated, law-abiding, and ethical in his conduct? He held high moral standards and, as we have noted, his religious sincerity was beyond question. But like the thief on the cross, he was lost because there is no salvation in sincerity.

Sincerity is of no value if you put your trust in your sincerity. On the other hand, if in honest sincerity one admits that his religious sincerity does not save and turns to the Savior, as Nicodemus did, such sincerity is to be praised. Nicodemus was so sincere about making his peace with God that when Jesus hit him with the profound statement, "Truly, truly, I say to you, unless one is born again, he cannot see the kingdom of God" (John 3:3), he didn't question the necessity of the new birth. His question wasn't "why" but *"how"* (John 3:4).

That night Nicodemus dropped his dependence upon his sincerity and good works, and the man who for many years had been "sincere but lost," was saved through faith in the One he secretly interviewed. "Whoever believes that Jesus is the Christ is born of God; and whoever loves the Father loves the *child* born of Him" (1 John 5:1). What human sincerity cannot do the divine Son of God can.

As Nicodemus was sincere, but lost, equally so, the idol worshiper is lost, no matter how sincere he may be. And he can only be saved as Nicodemus was saved—through a personal encounter with Jesus Christ.

CHAPTER 2

---◆---

THE LIGHT SWITCHED OFF

"Then God said, 'Let there be light'; and there was light . . . and God separated the light from the darkness. And God called the light day, and the darkness He called night . . . And God made the two great lights; the greater light to govern the day, and the lesser light to govern the night; He made the stars also. And *God placed them in the expanse of the heavens to give light on the earth,* and to govern the day and the night, and to separate the light from the darkness; and God saw that it was good" (Genesis 1:3–5, 16–18).

There is no problem with this truth unless one is an evolutionist. But our question relates to spiritual light. Does the person in the darkest corner of the earth have spiritual as well as physical light? Does the teen-ager of Tibet or the yet undiscovered tribesman in the jungles of Sumatra have spiritual light? If so, what is that light? How much does he have and does he possess enough spiritual light to make him responsible to God?

To answer such questions one must first ask: Is the Gospel the only light God has given to man? The Bible makes it abundantly clear the Gospel is

9

the most important light, because Jesus Christ is the complete revelation of God. But the Gospel is not the *only light.*

In the book of Romans, the Apostle Paul says that God has given spiritual light to all men. But man rejects that light and so becomes the object of God's righteous wrath: "For the wrath of God is revealed from heaven against all ungodliness and unrighteousness of men, who suppress the truth in unrighteousness" (Romans 1:18). Here God declares He has planted a germ of spiritual truth and light in the heart of all mankind. But man, through his unrighteousness, rejects, buries, and attempts to smother God's gift of light. This light is the light of God-consciousness which warns man of what is wrong and reveals what is right. But because of man's sinfulness, this God-awareness troubles him and he turns his back on it.

The Chinese idolater admits to God-consciousness. He speaks of the "Emperor above" or the "Supreme Emperor." All men everywhere, no matter how primitive, have their concept of a God or Spirit above all gods even though they may not worship Him.

The Scripture further states, "For even though they knew God, they did not honor Him as God, or give thanks; but they became futile in their speculations, and their foolish heart was darkened" (Romans 1:21). When one turns off the light, darkness results.

The Bible goes on to tell us what happens when the light is turned off: "Professing to be wise, they became fools, and exchanged the glory of the incorruptible God for an image in the form of corruptible man and of birds and four-footed animals and crawling creatures ... For all who have sinned without the Law will also perish without the Law; and all who have sinned under the Law will be judged by the Law; for not the hearers of the Law are just before God, but the doers of the Law will be justified. For when Gentiles who do not have the Law do instinctively the things of the Law, these, not having the Law, are a law to themselves, in that they show the work of the Law written in their hearts, their conscience bearing witness, and their thoughts alternately accusing or else defending themselves" (Romans 1:22, 23; 2:12–15). All men do not have the law of God written in a book (the Bible) but they do have it written in their hearts.

Is idolatry the result of man's search for a way to God? Some think it is, but let the heathen themselves answer that question. Those who are now converted tell me they resorted to religious ceremonies and idolatry to appease certain deities and evil spirits they feared. The fear stemmed from a sense of condemnation because they broke the divine laws written in their hearts. They admit God gave them an inner light, but confess they failed to live up to that light.

The work of the law written in their hearts is a light they choose to ignore. If that light does not reveal their sin and give them a sense of guilt, why then their sacrifices, pilgrimages, self-inflicted lacerations, and fasts?

The Scripture also states the heathen turn off another important light: "Because that which is known about God is evident within them; for God made it evident to them. For since the creation of the world His invisible attributes, His eternal power and divine nature, have been clearly seen, being understood through what has been made, so that they are without excuse" (Romans 1:19, 20).

It couldn't be clearer. God here states that creation, nature itself, is a light which points men to the power of His majesty and authority. Every man in every land possesses the "light of the knowledge of God" through His creation. As I watch a tribesman in the Highlands of Vietnam worship the spirit of a mountain stream or an animist in any land worship a tree, I know he is casting aside the testimony of natural theology. He has chosen to worship what God has created rather than worship the Creator.

Being in possession of the knowledge of the Creator through what He created makes man guilty if he in turn creates something and worships it. This, no doubt, is what Plato was confessing when he said, "The world must have a cause, and that cause is the Eternal Maker."

The Apostle Paul makes the testimony of creation clear when he states, "But I say, surely they have never heard, have they? Indeed they have: 'Their voice has gone out into all the earth, and their words to the ends of the world' " (Romans 10:18). Whose voice and whose words is it that goes forth to every tribe and nation? To find out we turn to the Psalm from which the apostle quotes: "The heavens are telling of the glory of God; And the firmament is declaring the work of His hands. Day to day pours forth speech, And night to night reveals knowledge. There is no speech, nor are there words; Their voice is not heard. Their line has gone out through all the earth, And their utterances to the end of the world. In them He has placed a tent for the sun" (Psalm 19:1–4).

All creation testifies to God's eternal power and deity. The refusal to accept this light leaves man without excuse. Within, there is divine awareness, God-consciousness; without, there is the awesome testimony of creation pointing to its Creator.

So we see God has written a law in the hearts of all men and they do, by nature, the things contained in the law. Then He gives them a conscience which enables them to interpret that law written in their hearts (see Romans 2:15). Disobedience to light always brings man under condemnation. All men have light and the rejection of that light makes them responsible. The measure of heathen responsibility is the measure of their light. Light creates responsibility.

For some there is yet a stronger spiritual light. God gave to the nation of Israel the testimony of the Law and the prophets. So clearly is the Lamb of God, the Messiah, revealed therein that if one accepts the words of the Old Testament prophets he will see the Savior. Christ proved this after His resurrection when He talked to two of His disciples: "And beginning with Moses and with all the prophets, He explained to them the things concerning Himself in all the Scriptures" (Luke 24:27).

At that time the New Testament had not been written. Nevertheless, Jesus makes it abundantly clear that there is enough light in the Old Testament *alone* to point man to God. But what did Israel do with God's light? For the most part she rejected it. Jesus puts the danger of rejection of spiritual light in full focus when He says, "And this is the judgment, that the light is come into the world, and men loved the darkness rather than the light; for their deeds were evil" (John 3:19).

If God in righteous judgment can condemn men who have rejected the light of God-awareness, the testimony of creation, and the word of the Law and the Prophets, how much greater will be the condemnation of those who turn their backs on Christ, the Light of the world. "How much severer punishment do you think he will deserve who has trampled under foot the Son of God, and has regarded as unclean the blood of the covenant by which he was sanctified, and has insulted the Spirit of grace?" (Hebrews 10:29).

I would rather face the judgment of God as a heathen, born and raised with no chance to hear the Gospel, than as an American who has lived and died rejecting the Gospel. Yes, in any case I would perish, but the judgment in the second case would be far greater than the first. This is the meaning of Paul's statement in Romans 2:12,

"For all who have sinned *without the Law* will also *perish without the Law;* and all who have sinned under the Law will be judged by the Law." Certainly the greater the light rejected the greater the condemnation expected.

All this looks as if heaven's population will be small and hell's overflowing. But do you know there are those who believe the reverse to be true? We will ferret out their reasoning in the next chapter.

CHAPTER 3

◆

LADDER OF STRAW

Whom will I meet in heaven? Will I meet my friend or neighbor whose conduct as I know it exemplifies Christ better than my own even though he has rejected the Savior? Will I meet Judas, or Nero, Marx, Stalin, or Mao? Will the good, bad, religious, and irreligious all meet in heaven? There are those who teach *all* will be there because they believe heaven is the ultimate destiny for *all* men. Yes, the universalist has built a stairway from earth to heaven which he claims all men will eventually climb.

It will do us good to attempt to ascend the universalist's staircase of straw. As you and I climb the stairs we will discover both the poor logic behind his arguments and the distortion of Scriptures he uses to defend his position. In the process we will note the Scriptures he deliberately chooses to ignore ... Scriptures which soundly refute his assumption that heaven is the ultimate destiny of all men.

It may surprise us to learn that the bottom step of this "ascent for all" is Scripture. The universalist uses (or misuses) the Word of God to defend his position. But in common with most heresies, the support texts are often taken out of context or misinterpreted. So the universalist accepts passages from Scripture that seem to prove his doctrine, but rejects those that don't. He keeps a long list of Bible verses on the subject of heaven, and cuts his list on hell as short as he dares. He emphasizes the eternalness of heaven but makes hell a kind of temporary purgatory.

To make his heresy authentic he boldly quotes Isaiah, our Lord Jesus, Paul, Peter, John, and others. Some examples are:

ISAIAH: "Then the glory of the Lord will be revealed, And *all* flesh will see it together" (Luke 3:6; Isaiah 40:5).

OUR LORD JESUS: "And I, if I be lifted up from the earth, will draw *all* men to Myself" (John 12:32).

PAUL: "Who desires *all* men to be saved and to come to the knowledge of the truth" (1 Timothy 2:4).

PAUL: "For it is for this we labor and strive, because we have fixed our hope on the living God, who is the Savior of *all* men ..." (1 Timothy 4:10).

PAUL: "For the grace of God has appeared, bringing salvation to *all* men" (Titus 2:11).

PAUL: "For as in Adam all die, so also in Christ *all* shall be made alive" (1 Corinthians 15:22).

PAUL: "And through Him to reconcile *all* things to Himself, having made peace through the blood of His cross ..." (Colossians 1:20).

PAUL: "... even so through one act of righteousness there resulted justification of life to *all* men" (Romans 5:18).

PETER: "Whom heaven must receive until the period of restoration of *all* things ..." (Acts 3:21).

PETER: "... not wishing for any to perish but for *all* to come to repentance" (2 Peter 3:9).

JOHN: "And He Himself is the propitiation for our sins; and not for ours only, but also for those of the *whole* world" (1 John 2:2).

Let's admit that the impact of the word "all" grows on one as each verse is studied. At the same time we must not be trapped into settling for fragmented half truth. The true seeker after truth must compare Scripture with Scripture.

Our desire to further search the Scriptures should be stimulated when we realize the same Savior who came "to seek and to save that which was lost" (Luke 19:10) is the very One who consistently warns of the dreadful danger of eternal punishment. Just as Christ refutes and rejects universalism, we too must choose to reject it. "I am the Truth," said Jesus, and we must follow Him.

The second step on the universalist's stairway of straw is his contention that the Christian is wrong in declaring that the Bible teaches a literal judgment and a *real* hell. To the universalist the idea of such punishment is pictorial rather than literal. However, we must again ask, "What did Jesus say?" "And if your hand causes you to stumble, cut it off; it is better for you to enter life crippled, than having your two hands" (Mark 9:43). Jesus makes judgment terribly real when He says it's better to cripple one's self than to face hell.

The third step to heaven on the universalist's stairway is the concept that there is no such thing as endless or eternal punishment. The universalist admits only to a temporary purgatory. Man, he says, goes to this purgatory of his own free will and may leave as soon as he repents.

But is this really what the Bible says? In speaking of future judgment, Jesus looks ahead to the days when He, as Judge of all the earth, will declare, "Depart from Me, accursed ones, into the eternal fire which has been prepared for the devil and his angels" (Matthew 25:41). "*Eternal* fire"—what frightening words! Yet they come from the lips of the compassionate Savior who died to save men from eternal punishment!

Before ascending the next step of this perilous stairway, let me say that all children of God must wholeheartedly accept the universal aspects of God's love and the finished work of Christ. "For God so loved the world" (John 3:16) is true. As is Philippians 2:10, 11: "That at the name of Jesus every knee should bow ... and every tongue should confess that Jesus Christ is Lord ..." But one must understand that although the claims of God mentioned above are universal and Christ's ultimate triumph will be universal, His saving grace is effective only to those who believe on Him (John 3:16, 18, 36; 1:12). Scripture must interpret Scripture. Christ talked just as clearly about eternal punishment as He did about eternal life. He spoke of the saved but also the lost; the blessed, but also the cursed!

The fourth step for the benign universalist is called *second chance*. If one does not hear the Gospel in this life, or if one hears but does not accept the gift of salvation—no matter. His sin, guilt, and punishment will ultimately be removed. The logic is that since Christ died for *all* He will sovereignly and out of love bring *all* men to heaven. How contrary this is to the words of our Lord, "He who believes in the Son has eternal life; but he who does not obey the Son shall not see life, but the wrath of God abides on him" (John 3:36).

The Apostle Paul agrees. He describes men as "children of wrath." He is referring to those who are appointed to wrath in the righteous judgment of God. As "all have sinned," as there is "none righteous, no, not one," all are therefore under the judgment and wrath of God. Just as the result of God's blessing is eternal life, so the result of God's wrath is eternal death. *Let us remember the wrath of God is only expressed where the extremity of human sin leaves God no other course.*

Also we must understand that nowhere does Scripture teach that man is given a second chance after death. Our Lord forever settled that question in His story about the rich man and Lazarus (Luke 16:19–31). Here Jesus makes it absolutely clear there is no second chance after death. There is *no* way to cross from the prison house of Sheol to the "courts of praise."

The top and last step might be named "sentimentality." The concept of eternal punishment, reasons the universalist, is immoral and since God is a God of love, there really is no hell. After all, how could God create a hell for beings He created and loves? Universalism further argues that since God is sovereign He must save all and since Christ died for all none can be lost.

The logical consequence of such reasoning is that salvation no longer becomes a matter of life and death but rather a choice of being saved *now* or *later*. It seems to me if salvation is more a convenience than a matter of life and death, then Calvary has lost its true meaning and Christ has become more a luxury than a necessity.

If the Christian does not possess a message—eternal life to gain and eternal death to fear—he has *no* message. Indeed, if universalism is true, the entire missionary activity of the Church is senseless. If universalism is true, why would the Apostle Paul exclaim almost in agony, "For woe is me if I do not preach the gospel" (1 Corinthians 9:16)? Why would he tell the Christians in Rome of his deep sense of debt and his urgent desire to pay that debt? "I am under obligation both to Greeks and to barbarians, both to the wise and to the foolish" (Romans 1:14). Why was he willing to bear such suffering in order to reach men and women with the Gospel?

"But in everything commending ourselves as servants of God, in much endurance, in afflictions, in hardships, in distresses, in beatings, in imprisonments, in tumults, in labors, in sleeplessness, in hunger ... Are they servants of Christ? (I speak as if insane) I more so; in far more labors, in far more imprisonments, beaten times without number, often in danger of death. Five times I received from the Jews thirty-nine lashes. Three times I was beaten with rods, once I was stoned, three times I was ship-wrecked, a night and a day I have spent in the deep. I have been on frequent journeys, in dangers from rivers, dangers from robbers, dangers from my countrymen, dangers from the Gentiles, dangers in the city, dangers in the wilderness, dangers on the sea, dangers among false brethren; I have been in labor and hardship, through many sleepless nights, in hunger and thirst, often without food, in cold and exposure" (2 Corinthians 6:4, 5; 11:23–27).

Indeed, why did Christ command His Church to carry "the Gospel to every creature" *in every nation in every generation?* Why should Christians pray for the salvation of the lost if it is already determined that all men will be saved? Why should believers give their substance for the spread of the Gospel if without the Gospel men will get to heaven? Why should Christians leave home and cross the seas? After all, what difference does it make *when* a man gets to heaven as long as he knows he will ultimately get there somehow, sometime?

There is a heaven and a hell. There are the saved and the lost. Scripture makes this plain. We must reach the lost that they might be saved. Heaven is not the ultimate destiny of all men. Those who come must come through Jesus Christ. He declares, ". . . no one comes to the Father, but through Me" (John 14:6).

CHAPTER 4

◆

I GOT RELIGION

All men have some form of religion. Men are, in fact, incurably religious. But does religion save? Does religion bring peace with God?

During my years in the Orient I talked with thousands of devotees of the great ethnic religions and found many to be deeply religious. But as I probed below the surface I discovered deep unrest.

"Do you work at your religion?" I asked.

"Yes."

"Do you feel your misdeeds are forgiven?"

"I cover them with my good deeds and offerings."

"Do you have fear about facing death?"

"Yes, I am afraid to die."

"Where will you go when you die?"

"I am not sure."

"Does your religion give you satisfaction of mind and joy of heart?"

"Not really, but I have nothing else."

"I have nothing else"—what tragic words! But are we to blame because they have *nothing else?* Let's answer this question by asking, "What is religion?"

Among other things, I believe religion is a ceremonial service caused by guilt and fear. It's Satan's counterfeit for salvation and a cover-up, not a blotting out of sin. It's the self-effort of man, not the saving grace of Jesus Christ. Religion leaves its devotee hoping for divine approval but never knowing; wishing but never certain.

I have been challenged for "imposing my *religion* on the people in the Orient." Invariably their objection is that America is a young upstart nation and Christianity, compared to other religions, is in its adolescence. The people of the Orient are proud of their rich religious heritage, art, poetry, and strong moral philosophy. Why destroy all this by imposing our Western religion? I have also been accused of destroying family unity and upsetting the lives of those to whom I have taken the Gospel. I have been told I was doing an injustice to people to come to them as a Christian missionary. I want you to know I wouldn't turn over in bed for religion . . . but I would circle the world for the sake of the Gospel!

I once asked one critic if he felt Christianity was just another religion like all the rest.

"Religions are like windows," he replied. "They may be different in size and shape but they all perform the same function. They let God's light in and they allow us to view God."

This is oversimplification. After all, man gets into heaven through a door, not a window. Jesus said, "I am the door; if anyone enters through Me, he shall be saved, and shall go in and out, and find pasture" (John 10:9).

To suggest that we not communicate the love of Christ to those who have not heard would indicate the Gospel has nothing to offer them. I believe Christianity has everything to offer religious man. From a spiritual standpoint, man has retrogressed rather than progressed in spite of his religious efforts. This clearly indicates that man's religious escalator only runs downward (Romans 1:23).

The dictionary classifies Christianity as a religion, but we must remember it's far more than that. Some schools teach a course called "Comparative Religions" and include Christianity among the many religions studied. This raises the question: Can one *compare* the Gospel with religion or do we find more truth in *contrasting* the two? My missionary friend, Dr. John T. Seamands, gives some powerful contrasts in his book, "The Supreme Task of the Church":

"Religion is man-made; the Gospel is God given.

"Religion is what man does for God; the Gospel is what God has done for man.

"Religion is man's search for God; the Gospel is God's search for man.

"Religion is good views; the Gospel is Good News.

"Religion is good advice; the Gospel is a glorious announcement.

"Religion takes man and leaves him as he is; the Gospel takes a man as he is and makes him what he ought to be.

"Religion ends in an outer reformation; the Gospel ends in an inner transformation.

"Religion whitewashes; the Gospel washes white.

"Religion places the prime emphasis upon doing; the Gospel places the emphasis on a Person.

"You can take Buddha out of Buddhism and Buddhism still remains with its four noble truths and its eight-fold path.

"You can take Mohammed out of Islam and Islam is still intact with its five pillars of action and its six articles of belief.

"But if you take Christ out of the Gospel there is nothing left, for the Gospel is Christ."

Christianity is a *life*—the life of Christ implanted in the heart of man. Christianity is unique in that it alone has a living Author. No religion dare claim this distinction.

In the heart of China stands a large ornate Confucian temple. The main courtyard surrounds a mound of dirt over sixty feet high. Yearly, thousands burn incense before that mound. They believe the skull of Confucius is buried beneath the pyramid of dirt. It may well be, for the founders of all the great ethnic religions are dead.

I have not visited Mecca but millions of ardent Muslims have. Why? To pay their respects to the remains of Mohammed, the founder of the Muslim religion. Of man, God said, "For you are dust, and to dust you shall return" (Genesis 3:19). The dust of Mohammed remains in Mecca.

Not long ago I visited an empty tomb in Jerusalem. Is it the actual tomb in which the body of

Christ was placed by Joseph and Nicodemus? One must not be dogmatic. But the Christian is positive that Christ conquered death and the grave. He arose from the grave, broke the Roman seal, shoved the great stone aside and ascended into heaven. This is the uniqueness of Christianity. Christ came to save men from sin and religion. And one of the powerful proofs of His Saviorhood is the empty tomb.

For millions of people religion is little more than a security blanket. If you doubt this take an informal poll and ask each person if they are a Christian? You will discover a variety of answers. "I get to church as often as I can." "I go to church every Christmas and Easter." "I don't swear, drink, or smoke." Others who are asked this question raise their voices and emphasize the strength of their religious conviction with, "What do you think I am, a pagan?"

Such mistaken attitudes did not begin with the *now generation*. Religion was born in a beautiful garden millenniums ago: ". . . And they (Adam and Eve) sewed fig leaves together and made themselves loin coverings" (Genesis 3:7). Our first parents attempted to cover their disobedience and sin by their own efforts and this is exactly what "religion" is all about. Apart from the intervention of God, man's way will always be the way of fig leaves—works and religion. Wise Solomon reminds us, "There is a way which seems right to a man, But its end is the way of death" (Proverbs 14:12).

Who better illustrates the difference between

religion and salvation than Adam's first-born son, Cain? (See Genesis 4:3-5.) Cain was no different than most of us. He felt the need of doing something to please God. He possessed an inner consciousness of a holy God. He experienced deep guilt because of conduct he knew was wrong in the sight of God. As a religious man he searched for a way to quiet his constant awareness of guilt. Cain was religious.

The Bible says, "So it came about in the course of time that Cain brought an offering to the Lord of the fruit of the ground" (Genesis 4:3). Cain possessed real convictions about a man's duty toward a holy God and came up with the idea of appeasing God with an offering from his fields.

Today the vast majority of mankind follows Cain's example. The heart of their religion is offerings of fruit, rice, incense, and good works.

One does not question the sincerity of Cain. Remember, he did not murder his brother until after his self-devised religion had failed. Nor does one question the sincerity of many who are involved in the thousands of sects, cults, isms, and religious creeds of today. If sincerity alone could save, there is little question that many religious people would be saved. But sincerity alone is not enough. Just as one can be sincere and sincerely right, so one can be sincere and sincerely *wrong*.

Adam's first-born, Cain, was sincerely wrong even if we grant him the quality of sincerity. Cain was no agnostic. He believed in God. And it would seem he believed in salvation, even if it was a fig leaf, an "I-must-save-myself" salvation—a salvation of works. And that is the cornerstone of all religion.

It would be incongruous for Adam not to teach his sons that God, not man, is the Author of true salvation. Had he not told his sons that God ripped off the fig leaves of personal effort? Certainly he reported to Cain and Abel that the skins they now wore were provided by God through the death of an innocent substitute. How would younger brother Abel know this without older brother Cain's knowledge? Cain's problem was that he was religious, proud, self-sufficient, and unbelieving about God's way of salvation.

In many ways Cain's offering was more attractive than Abel's. Who wants to stare at a lifeless bleeding lamb? Isn't golden grain more appealing? Yes, let's admit some religions have areas of remarkable beauty. But beauty does not save. God saw in Abel's lamb the figure of the coming "Lamb of God" who would take away the sin of the world. In Cain's offering of grain God saw the beginning of man's efforts to save himself.

Is it possible to follow religious rites and be lost? A thousand times, yes! Religion (man's works) has never opened the door of heaven to a single soul. All men without the Lamb of God are lost.

Religion is Satan's counterfeit for God's salvation. Christianity is God's answer to Satan's religions.

CHAPTER 5

◆

"I COULD HAVE TOUCHED GOD"

Is it possible to be within arm's reach of Christ and yet be lost? The answer to this question is found in a backward look at two men.

One was near Christ by choice; the other was near Him through circumstance. One was near Him in life; the other was near Him in death. One man was near Him for almost three years; the other was near Him for a few short hours. One was a chosen disciple; the other a nameless thief.

Today one of those *near* men is with Christ. The other *near* man is separated by an immeasurable distance in eternal death and doom. Near, very near, but very lost. Being near is not enough.

First we look at the nameless thief. Roman soldiers nailed Jesus to a cross and the thief hung there almost within arm's reach of Christ. "And he was saying, 'Jesus, remember me when You come in Your kingdom!' And He (Jesus) said to him, 'Truly I say to you, today you shall be with Me in Paradise'" (Luke 23:42, 43).

Let's take a longer look at the other man, a chosen disciple, who lived most of three years with the Savior. We are told that Jesus chose him along with eleven other men. From this we conclude that Judas chose to be near Jesus. Could anyone be closer to Jesus than living with Him as His disciple?

There are those who suggest that Judas, motivated by patriotism, became a disciple to help deliver Israel from Roman oppression. The Scripture, however, does not bear this out. Rather the study of his life shows he was an ambitious opportunist and was out to get all he could for himself. If Jesus were the hoped-for Messiah, then Judas could only gain by being one of the first disciples. This he believed would assure him of a place in Messiah's cabinet.

He was clever enough to fully consider the cost of following Christ. He could be religious enough to fool the wisest and, at the same time, keep his religion subservient to his lust for power and position. He was godly only for personal gain. His very act of following Christ was cool, planned, and deliberate. His aim was his own personal aggrandizement.

We get a vivid picture of human depravity and deceit by watching Judas. To accomplish its selfish purposes, human depravity is willing to clothe itself in the sacred profession of the clergy. It is prepared to join in the holiest of companionship and to live under the brilliant glare of the clearest of Light.

No man ever acted his part as well as Judas. He prayed with the devotion of a George Mueller and preached with the fervor of a Billy Sunday. He was so like the other "world changers" that not one of them put a finger of suspicion on him. Not until the night of his betrayal did his fellow disciples know their constant companion was a hypocrite. On that night, Judas joined the other disciples in asking with seeming amazement, "Surely it is not I, Rabbi?" (Matthew 26:25). What indescribable hypocrisy! By now, his hypocrisy was a fixed law of his being. Judas was its slave. It would destroy him as it can surely destroy us today.

This dangerous hypocrisy is easy to recognize in the "two timers" who attend church only on Christmas and Easter, but more difficult to see among those who profess to faithfully serve Him. Yet, if one is honest, hypocrisy is not difficult to uncover. Have you ever asked yourself: "Why did I do that? Why did I say that? Was I completely honest or was I trying to impress?"

Christ hates hypocrisy and judges it sternly. No less than eight times in the twenty-third chapter of Matthew we read, "Woe unto you, scribes and Pharisees, hypocrites!" Jesus closes His pronouncements of judgment on the hypocrite by asking a searching question, "How shall you escape the sentence of hell?" (Matthew 23:33). Is it any wonder that Judas, the master hypocrite, is called "son of perdition"?

Judas' heart was filled not only with hypocrisy but also covetousness. The Scriptures plainly teach that covetousness is idolatry. And while Judas walked with God he served idols. It is not strange that he sought and got the job of treasurer of the company. His greed became apparent when he rebuked Mary with crass words for wasting her love offering of spikenard-ointment on the feet of Jesus. Hypocrite that he was, he suggested the ointment should have been sold and the money used for the poor. No doubt the disciples agreed with Judas, but the Savior put His finger on Judas' wicked heart. John 12:6 says, "Now he said this, not because he was concerned about the poor, but because he was a thief, and as he had the money box, he used to pilfer what was put into it."

So frustrated was Judas in his attempt to get the three hundred pence, that he plotted to sell his Lord for thirty pieces of silver. He was not the last man who betrayed his Lord for money. Today millions make materialism their god. They pay no attention to the question, "For what will a man be profited, if he gains the whole world, and forfeits his soul? Or what will a man give in exchange for his soul?" (Matthew 16:26).

As Christians you and I face the constant danger of dividing our affections between God and mammon. The Word of God warns, "You shall have no other gods before Me" (Exodus 20:3). It is our responsibility to judge and cast down the idol of materialism.

Though near to Christ, Judas did not at any time show he was a man of faith. His heart was filled with unbelief. To doubt is dreadful, but doubt may be born of honest intellectual difficulty. However, this was not Judas' problem. His was a problem not of mind, but of will.

For three years he had been given solid evidence that Christ was the Son of God. But by an act of his will *refused* to accept this evidence. This is that "wicked heart of unbelief" spoken of in the Scriptures. And because it was immoral and unbelief at its worst, it destroyed him. All of Judas' sins could be forgiven, but persistent unbelief leads only to destruction. You and I cannot afford to overlook the danger of allowing unbelief to lurk in some hidden corner of our hearts.

For nearly three years Jesus dealt patiently and graciously with Judas. He knew Judas for the "man of sin" he was, yet He loved him and gave him every chance to repent. In the great Bread of Life discourse, Christ revealed to His disciples and us that He is the Living Bread from heaven. He invited all to partake and live. Near the close of His message, our Lord aimed a warning directly at Judas, " 'But there are some of you who do not believe.' For Jesus knew from the beginning who they were who did not believe, and who it was that would betray Him" (John 6:64). Judas hardened his heart and *refused* to acknowledge his unbelief. That's double jeopardy!

Many of the multitude who heard the Bread of Life discourse refused to accept its truth and turned from Christ. The Lord, seeing what was happening, turned to the twelve and asked them what they wanted to do. Acting as spokesman, Peter said, "And we have believed and have come to know that You are the Holy One of God" (John

6:69). In using the "we" it's evident the disciples were unaware of the unbelief in Judas' heart. Peter was confident he was speaking for all.

But Jesus knew differently and plainly answered Peter by saying, "Did I myself not choose you, the twelve, and yet one of you is a devil?" John adds, "Now He meant Judas the son of Simon Iscariot, for he, one of the twelve, was going to betray Him" (John 6:70, 71). Judas felt the finger of God upon him but hardened his heart.

Just before His crucifixion Christ met with the twelve in the Upper Room. After their supper, Jesus began to wash His disciples' feet. None objected until He came to Peter. "If I do not wash you," said Jesus, "you have no part with Me" (John 13:8). Not fully aware of what He meant, Peter requested Jesus to also wash his hands and head. Jesus' answer to Peter was another attempt to warn Judas and allow him to repent: " 'He who has bathed needs only to wash his feet, but is completely clean; and you are clean, but not all of you.' For He knew the one who was betraying Him; for this reason He said, 'Not all of you are clean' " (John 13:10, 11). Only Judas understood what Jesus was talking about. Yet he hardened his heart. So *near* but so *lost*!

That same evening Jesus startled the twelve by saying to them, "Truly, truly, I say to you, that one of you will betray Me" (John 13:21). This is an opportunity for Judas to cry out in repentance and confession. Yet his silence tells the story—he again hardens his heart in unbelief. Things move rapidly now. Prodded by Peter, John bluntly asks, "Lord, who is it?" For the first time Jesus exposes Judas. " 'That is the one for whom I shall dip the morsel, and give it to him.' So when He had dipped the morsel, He took and gave it to Judas, the son of Simon Iscariot." Now come those frightening words, "Satan then entered into him" (John 13:25, 26, 27).

Jesus and Judas meet once again in the Garden of Gethsemane. Judas, now turned traitor, greets his Lord with a kiss. Jesus, merciful to the end, gives Judas one final demonstration of His power and love. Lovingly protecting His frightened disciples, Jesus Christ asks the priests and soldiers whom they seek. "We have come to arrest Jesus of Nazareth," they reply. As Jesus answers them, He majestically uses His divine title, "I AM." Overcome by the authority with which He speaks that holy name, they fall on their faces. This is indeed a moment for Judas to repent. But again he *refuses* Christ's love and mercy.

It is frighteningly possible for one to be within arm's reach of the Savior and still be lost. And is being "lost" all that terrible? We will seek the answer in the following chapter.

CHAPTER 6

◆

WALK THROUGH A GRAVEYARD

Walk through any cemetery and notice the size of each grave—some are short, others long. As one looks at a little grave, a picture of a child flashes across the mental screen. The baby's time on earth was so short!

On a larger stone the inscription reads, "Born 1903, died 1973." We observe he lived a long life, a full seventy years. Long—compared to what? Compared to the child, *yes*. Compared to eternity, *no*. At best, life on earth is short. At its longest and *happiest* life is only a burst of music on a crowded street. At its longest and *saddest* it is a quick sigh in the dark.

Job observed, "Man, who is born of woman, Is short-lived and full of turmoil. Like a flower he comes forth and withers. He also flees like a shadow and does not remain" (14:1, 2). The Apostle Peter wrote, "For, all flesh is like grass, And all its glory like the flower of grass. The grass withers, And the flower falls off" (1 Peter 1:24).

Where do we go from here? What lies beyond the cemetery? Important questions! Questions that have been asked for generations and demand answers. Where are those who have died?

Is the grave the end of all things? If so, isn't life a poor joke, a stupid mistake, a mockery?

To ignore such questions won't change the facts. Life is short and death is sure, "And inasmuch as it is appointed for men to die once, and after this comes judgment" (Hebrews 9:27). After death, what? After death—judgment!

Mankind knows death is not the end. Belief in an immortality is almost universal. Several times every year millions of people in the Orient visit the graveside of departed loved ones. They bring food offerings, paper horse-drawn carts and "hell" money. The cart, horse, and money are burned. Why? They say, "As the smoke ascends, the departed spirit uses the horse-drawn cart for transportation. He uses the 'hell' money to carry on his eternal existence."

Others teach that after death all are finally absorbed into one universal "personality" (pantheism). Millions more believe in many reincarnations and the transmigration of the eternal soul of man. No matter what, in all cases they believe there is some form of continuing existence after death.

Centuries ago, Job asked, "If a man dies, will he live again?" (14:14). Since then, many have argued, discussed, and risked a calculated guess. But did not Jesus put the question to rest when He said, "Do not marvel at this; for an hour is coming, in which all who are in the tombs shall hear His voice, and shall come forth; those who did the good deeds, to a resurrection of life, those who committed the evil deeds to a resurrection of judgment" (John 5:28, 29). To the question, "After death, what?" Jesus answers that "*all* shall hear His voice," *all* from the beginning of time, *all* from the first man to the last.

The thought that sobers one is that after so brief a life there follows an endless eternity. The future is forever—but where? Jesus makes it clear that men will spend eternity in one of two places. Some will spend eternity in God's house—heaven. Others will live forever in hell, yes, a literal hell. Every soul ever born into this world is destined to live for eternity. And every time the clock ticks, a soul is ushered into that eternity.

Recently I followed the casket of a loved one to a cemetery. I stood by the grave and asked, "What happens to a person at the moment of death?" When I returned home, I went to the Bible in search of the answer and here is what I found. The body goes back to the earth to decay between death and resurrection, ". . . For you are dust, And to dust you shall return" (Genesis 3:19). Moses said, "Thou dost turn man back into dust . . ." (Psalm 90:3). The Psalmist writes, ". . . Thou dost take away their spirit (breath), they expire, And return to their dust" (Psalm 104:29).

Up to the time of the ascension of Jesus, the souls of both the saved and the lost went into Sheol, a place of suffering for the lost, a place of peace and rest "in Abraham's bosom" for those who died in faith. (Sheol is the Hebrew word, Hades the Greek word, for the same place. The clearest picture of this is given in Luke 16:19–23.)

On the cross Jesus cried, "Father, into Thy

hands I commit My spirit" (Luke 23:46). His body died and was placed in the grave, but His spirit went into Sheol (New Testament, Hades). Then on the day of His resurrection He led believers triumphantly into heaven. Since then all who have died "in faith" go directly into the presence of God. Therefore, Paul boldly states, "we are of good courage, I say, and prefer rather to be absent from the body and to be at home with the Lord" (2 Corinthians 5:8).

The wicked dead, both before and after Calvary, are in Sheol. There they live in conscious torment. From a study of Numbers 16:28–35, I believe Sheol (or Hades) is somewhere in the heart of the earth. The Apostle Paul also indicates this when he writes, "Now this expression, 'He ascended,' what does it mean except that He also had descended into the lower parts of the earth?" (Ephesians 4:9).

But what about those who die without faith? Bluntly, they are lost—lost to God, because each went his own way. If a person who lived without faith in Christ is now dead, his body decays in the ground. His soul waits in conscious torment in Hades until the Great White Throne Judgment. At that time he will be cast into hell, which is also called "the lake of fire and brimstone" (Revelation 20:10).

I must stop long enough to point out *one* exception. If a little child dies, whether of Christian or non-Christian parents, his spirit returns to God. The prophet Samuel helps throw light on this subject. He records King David's deep sorrow as for seven days he fasts, prays, and watches his new-born baby grow weaker. After his baby died the Scripture says, "So David arose from the ground, washed, anointed himself, and changed his clothes; and he came into the house of the Lord and worshiped" (2 Samuel 12:20). His servants were surprised and questioned his conduct. King David gave them a logical answer: "But now he has died; why should I fast? Can I bring him back again? I shall go to him, but he will not return to me" (2 Samuel 12:23). King David had confidence that the same God who created the child, called him home to Himself. He knew, therefore, he would see his child again.

In my opinion, the strong words of Christ take care of all who die in infancy. They came from God and they return to God. In many countries infant mortality is extremely high. Our Chinese cook, for example, had nine children. Seven of them died during infancy. Where are those children? They, like unnumbered millions of others, are in heaven.

Hell is in the vocabulary of many people. And, wouldn't you know it, those who use it most often fear it least! Many who find it impossible to answer a question without a "Hell, yes" or "Hell, no" don't believe there is such a place. But hell is a place as real as Shanghai or San Francisco. It is the awful eternal address of all those who have not personally responded to Jesus Christ.

And what is this place called hell like? Hell is a place of remembering and regretting. It's a place of seeing, desiring, and finding it unattainable. Hell is the eternal absence of God and the eternal presence of the Devil and his demons. Hell is a place of hopelessness and of forfeiting everything forever.

Does the word *"lost"* take on new meaning for you now? It should! Remember, there is no question whether men *will* be lost. Every child is born into a lost world. His first cry is made in a lost state. His first breath is taken in an atmosphere of lostness. He is without God, without a Mediator, without a Savior, without the Way, and he is lost. The only way he can find his way is by being saved.

Let me make a confession. When I first approached the subject of lostness, I faced a natural emotional barrier. Like you, I desire no one to be eternally separated from God. In a special way I want all who have never heard to be saved. I would like to shout from the housetop that they are not lost.

How much less responsibility I, as a Christian, would feel toward those in pagan lands if I could prove that even in their lives apart from Christ they would somehow get to heaven. On the other hand, if the Scriptures show they are eternally lost, "without God and without hope," how grave is my responsibility!

If the heathen are not lost, the birth of Christ is of little significance. At the time of His birth it was announced, "And she will bear a Son; and you shall call His name Jesus, for it is He who will save His people from their sins" (Matthew 1:21).

That this salvation was not limited to the Jews

is clear. When the aged Simeon beheld the Christ Child, he said, "For mine eyes have seen Thy salvation, Which Thou hast prepared in the presence of all peoples, A light of revelation to the Gentiles, And the glory of Thy people Israel" (Luke 2:30–32).

Furthermore, the angel of the Lord said to the shepherds, "Do not be afraid; for behold, I bring you good news of a great joy which shall be for all the people" (Luke 2:10).

Later on, when John the Baptist introduced Christ to his followers, he said, "Behold, the Lamb of God who takes away the sin of the world!" (John 1:29). Salvation is for all because all are lost.

If the heathen are not really lost, then many of the teachings of Christ become absurd. The familiar verse, "For God so loved the world, that He gave His only begotten Son, that whoever believes in Him should not perish, but have eternal life" (John 3:16), is totally without import if men and women without Christ are not lost.

And how can we explain such a statement as, "For God did not send the Son into the world to judge the world; but that the world should be saved through Him" (John 3:17), except on the basis of the world's need of salvation?

Or how are Christ's claims to be the "Light of the *world*" and the "Bread of life" to be understood, apart from the fact that men are walking in spiritual darkness and spiritual famine?

If the heathen are not lost, Christ's post-resurrection and pre-ascension commands to His disciples are a mockery. In Luke 24:47, He commands "that repentance for forgiveness of sins should be proclaimed in His name to *all* the nations—beginning from Jerusalem."

Christ's last words given to His followers, in Acts 1:8, read, "but you shall receive power when the Holy Spirit has come upon you; and you shall be My witnesses both in Jerusalem, and in all Judea and Samaria, and even to the remotest part of the earth."

These verses might well be stricken from the Scriptures if men without Christ are not lost.

If the heathen are not really lost, then the Lord was in error when He said to His disciples, "Peace be with you; as the Father has sent Me, I also send you" (John 20:21). Why did the Father send Him? Jesus Himself answers, "For the Son of Man has come to seek and to save that which was lost" (Luke 19:10).

The Gospel does not keep men from becoming lost. Rather the Good News, like a beam of light, searches out the lost and brings them to God through Christ. The salvation of the Gospel has meaning only if the wrath of God spoken of in the Gospels is man's eternal doom. Wrath and doom, separation and hell, are not easy words for one to utter.

An important part of the Gospel is the unflinching presentation of the lost condition of all. God must be allowed to be God. We dare not play at being God. We weep over those who rush to their own destruction. We cry *for* the lost. We cry *to* the lost. We must *do all* to *tell all* of Christ's salvation *for all*. We must, that is, if Christ alone can save lost men. We dare not stop here. We must move on to the next chapter to find out if there is really only *one* way.

CHAPTER 7

◆

ONLY ONE WAY!

In some youth circles it is popular to raise the right arm and while pointing the index finger toward heaven to cry, "One way." What do these young people mean by this gesture and shout? Their act is symbolic. They mean there is only one way to obtain salvation and one road to heaven. And what is that *one way?* It is faith in Christ.

All this may be fine if one is a Christian. But Christians are a small percentage of the world's population. What if one is a Hindu? A Buddhist? A Muslim? Each believes he has his own way of obtaining salvation and gaining heaven. Before we conclude, therefore, that there is but one way, "our way," remember we are outnumbered.

Five hundred million Hindus have *their* heaven and *their* way of reaching it. Their salvation consists of "losing one's ego and individuality even as a river loses its name and form when it flows into the ocean." To the Hindu all life comes from God and flows to God. "God is all and all is God," they say. Therefore, their way is to worship anything and everything in nature.

Furthermore, the Hindu bases his faith on scriptures he feels are more reliable than ours.

He is firmly convinced the words of Krishna are more consistent with faith in a merciful, loving, divine author than anything you and I have in the Bible. To the Hindu, the impression left by Christian missionary evangelism is one of self-righteousness and egotism. And to the sincere Hindu nothing is more irreligious than a holier-than-thou attitude. Dare we still insist on "one way"? Then how about the Hindu way?

Today Buddhism holds sway over millions of Orientals. For the Buddhist devotee there is also a "heaven" and a way to get there. Their way of salvation is a paradox. It is at one and the same time a long tortuous journey filled with suffering and struggle against sensual things, and a short eight-step path from darkness to light. To reach heaven, the place of "restful peace," involves a studied turn to the right: (1) right views, (2) right resolves, (3) right speech, (4) right action, (5) right living, (6) right effort, (7) right mindfulness, and (8) right concentration. Do we still insist on "one way"? Then how about the Buddhist way?

Biblical Christians believe there is only one way and that way is faith in Christ. But what about the millions who place implicit faith in a man who came some five hundred years after Christ? Since his birth his powerful influence on many in every generation can hardly be over-estimated. His name was Mohammed, the founder of the Muslim religion. He claimed that all he wrote in the Koran was received through divine revelation. Mohammed clearly proclaimed a way of salvation and pointed a way to heaven. Submission is "the way." His Koran says God is sovereign and man has no choice but to submit. In such submission is man's salvation, and salvation is the gateway to heaven. If we still insist on *one way*—our way—are those of the Muslim religion lost?

There is more than one way to get from California to Florida. You can go by boat through the Canal, drive a car, ride a bus, or fly. So what's in a name? Call him Jehovah, Shiva, Allah, Jesus, or Buddha. Isn't He still God?

To find the answer we are driven to the authentic source of authority—the Bible. What does Scripture teach? What did Jesus say about Himself? Preceding His death on the cross, Jesus told His faithful followers that He was leaving them to go to His Father's house. He could have said, "I am going to heaven," for heaven is "His Father's house" (John 14). He further assured them that after preparing a place for them He would return for them. When His disciple, Thomas, asked to know the way, Jesus replied, "I am *the* way." Jesus did not say, "I am a way," or, "I am one of many ways," but, "I am *the* way." To make His point and prove He is the only way, He adds, "no one comes to the Father, but through Me" (John 14:6).

Remember the Father's house is heaven. So He could have said, "*No* one enters heaven, but through Me." Christ's claim for Himself is clear: "I am the only means of salvation. I am the only way to heaven." Jesus had the same profound truth in mind when He spoke these simple words,

"I am the door; if anyone enters through Me, he shall be saved, and shall go in and out, and find pasture" (John 10:9). His Father's house (heaven) has a door and He is that Door. Therefore, to get inside the house one must go through Him.

The first disciples were willing to lay their lives on the line to defend this important truth. Paul felt he had no right to surrender the uniqueness of Christ. So certain was he that Christ was the only Way that he cried, "For woe is me if I do not preach the gospel" (1 Corinthians 9:16). Paul thought of himself as owing the whole world a tremendous debt. He saw mankind as doomed by the deadly disease of sin and knew Christ to be the only way of salvation. "I am under obligation both to Greeks and to barbarians, both to the wise and to the foolish" (Romans 1:14). Could any words more eloquently express the apostle's conviction that Christ holds the only cure for sin and therefore the only way into the presence of an infinite God?

Peter expresses the same high sense of obligation. Soon after Christ's ascension, we find the once fearful Peter standing before the religious elite in Jerusalem: "Annas the high priest was there, and Caiaphas and John and Alexander, and all who were of high-priestly descent" (Acts 4:6). Peter is on trial for proclaiming the resurrection of Jesus Christ. The once cowardly Peter now courageously and fearlessly declares, "And there is salvation in no one else; for there is no other name under heaven that has been given among men, by which we must be saved" (Acts 4:12).

Note those powerful words, "no one else" and "no other name." Prophets there are. Holy men there may be. But there is "no one else" but Jesus Christ who can save. He is the only Door; He is the only Way.

"For there is one God, and one mediator also between God and men, the man Christ Jesus" (1 Timothy 2:5). The Word of God leaves no doubt that there is only "one way."

Is the question settled or are there still honest doubts about the "one way"? If so, could it be because of our low view of sin? Have *all* men sinned? Is the fruit of sin separation from God? Then are not all men separated? Think of such words as self, self-seeking, self-defense, self-indulgence, self-justification and self-righteousness. One can add a hundred other words that spell sin in any man's language. "How," I ask, "can this universal sin question be adequately dealt with?" I am forced back to the "one way."

Jesus said, "And I, if I be lifted up from the earth, will draw all men to Myself" (John 12:32). His words become a highway of faith on which man can travel from sin to salvation. Through His moral grandeur, His perfection, His majesty, His love for sinners, His obedience to God, His challenge, "Which one of you convicts Me of sin?" (John 8:46), and His Father's testimony, "This is My beloved Son, with whom I am well pleased; hear Him!" (Matthew 17:5), we are forced to cast doubts aside and declare, "What God has spoken I believe. Christ is the only Way! Apart from Christ there is no other Good News!"

Listen to Paul the great missionary apostle: "But even though we, or an angel from heaven, should preach to you a gospel contrary to that which we have preached to you, let him be accursed" (Galatians 1:8).

CHAPTER 8

◆

IS GOD CRUEL?

A personal friend once looked me in the eye and said, "When I look at suffering in the world I cannot believe in a God of love. To me God is cruel."

Dr. Richard Halverson handles this statement by saying, "Very well, assume there is no God of love, what changes? Suffering doesn't! You don't get rid of suffering by denying a God of love. You don't even make suffering more bearable. If the Scripture is false in its portrayal of a God of infinite justice, love, mercy, and righteousness, the last vestige of reason and hope is gone."

The Bible says, "God is love." What does that mean? Does love punish? Can love act unjustly? If God loves His creatures, why is there a hell? Did God create it?

Scripture does not hide the fact that God created hell. At the same time, the Bible makes it clear that hell was never meant for man but "for the devil and his angels" (Matthew 25:41). Somewhere along the line man rejects light, sides with the god of this world (see 2 Corinthians 4:4) and refuses heaven.

"God is love" is not simply a nice-sounding

Judeo-Christian proverb. It is a fact. Because God is love He created a heaven and a hell. In love God has provided all that is necessary for all men everywhere to be delivered from condemnation. The death of His Son on the cross is sufficient proof of this. "And He Himself is the propitiation for our sins; and not for ours only, but also for those of the whole world" (1 John 2:2). God, in unsurpassed love, executed judgment upon His own Son. "He made Him who knew no sin to be sin on our behalf, that we might become the righteousness of God in Him" (2 Corinthians 5:21). God has declared, "The wages of sin is death" (Romans 6:23). Through His death, Christ paid the righteous demands of a just and holy God.

The Apostle Peter puts the love of God for His creatures in right perspective when he declares, "The Lord is not slow about His promise, as some count slowness, but is patient toward you, not wishing for *any* to perish but for *all* to come to repentance" (2 Peter 3:9). Not *any*—not even the lowest. The Judases, Neros, Hitlers, Maos—He loves their eternal souls and longs that all should be saved. The Psalmist puts it this way: "The Lord is gracious and merciful; Slow to anger and great in lovingkindness" (Psalm 145:8).

And then there is that incomprehensible statement in the third chapter of the Gospel of John: "For God so loved the *world*." Incomprehensible because the world is so dark, dirty, and unlovable. Is not an honest man forced to conclude that God must be a God of love to love such a depraved, crazy, sinful, often God-hating world?

God's love is strongly proved in the thoughtful way He created all men with the inner light of God consciousness. His love is further demonstrated in the outer light of His magnificent creation which points every man to the Creator. And nowhere is His love more clearly seen and distinctly heard than when Jesus, hanging on the cross, cried, "My God, My God, why hast Thou forsaken Me?" (Matthew 27:46). The only answer to the dying Christ's penetrating question is that God so loved His creatures He allowed His Son to bear their punishment that they might be reconciled to Him. Is this not what Paul boldly declares to the believers in Corinth? "He made Him who knew no sin to be sin on our behalf, that we might become the righteousness of God in Him" (2 Corinthians 5:21).

Another point needs to be made: Love that is not voluntary is not true love. Forced love is counterfeit love. A present-day theologian argues that God's love will pursue every man until he is reconciled. Nonsense! Part of the dignity of man is that he can say "no" to God. One of the strongest arguments for the love of God is that He created man with a free will. Man would simply be a robot had he been created without the privilege of choice. The freedom of the human will, therefore, testifies clearly to God's love.

God desires companionship with a creature who has the power to accept or reject that companionship. Therefore, in love He created us with the power of choice (see Genesis 1:26, 27). In infinite love and justice God allows every man the right to choose between rebelling against Him or living in fellowship with Him.

There are things in Scripture we may not understand, but of this we can be sure—God is love, and He is just!

But how does one define and understand the unfathomable depths of God's love? No man has lived, or ever will, who fully comprehends the love of God. As I have stated, God's love in its most brilliant form is seen in Jesus Christ!

To help believers in Ephesus see this love, the Apostle Paul spoke of the four dimensions of Christ's love—breadth, length, depth, height (see Ephesians 3:17–19). In incredible love Christ left the highest heaven and went to the lowest hell for us.

Can the *breadth* and *width* of Christ's love be measured? How does one measure something that is infinite? Human language is inadequate. King David comes closest when he writes, "As far as the east is from the west, so far has He removed our transgressions from us" (Psalm 103:12). To David the width of the love of God is all-encompassing and absolutely immeasurable.

And how does one define the *length* of the love of God in Christ? Since God is love and God has no beginning or end, then it follows that God's love is beginningless and endless.

Why during His crucifixion did Jesus cry, "My God, My God, why hast Thou forsaken Me?" The answer is not difficult. Christ, in His love for lost man, volunteered to pay the consequences of man's sin. Bearing those sins on His own body on the cross He was separated from God, died, and went to Hades. If it were possible to multiply the agony of Christ's separation from the Father by eternity, we would understand more fully two great truths. First, we would see the awfulness of being eternally separated from the Father. Second, we would understand to what *depth* the sinless Son of God went to keep men out of hell. Christ's love reached low enough to reach the lowest.

And what about the *height* of God's love? Human words are too frail and inadequate to describe it. Only when man has experienced heaven will he fully appreciate the height to which God's love has carried him.

Why love with such immeasurable measurements? Because sinful, unworthy, hell-deserving creatures are lovable? Never! God loves mankind because God is infinite love without beginning and without end.

Man's Future Is Forever...
...so WHAT?

PART II

---◆---

We no longer say "*if* men are lost."

We know from the clear statements of Scripture that all mankind is separated from God by sin.

We know that only through the life, atoning death, and resurrection of Jesus Christ is redemption possible.

We know we are in this world to witness to the Lordship of Christ by offering to all men of "every tribe and tongue and people and nation" the Good News of God's saving love in Christ.

We know God's purpose is for every believer to be involved in making it possible for every man to hear this Good News.

We also know millions of Christians are indifferent to this God-appointed responsibility.

In the following chapters we ask pointed searching questions in an effort to put a finger on this failure so as to come up with practical remedies. At times it will hurt but like removing a cancer, it becomes the kind of hurt that makes us healthy.

CHAPTER 9

◆

SOME SINS ARE NICER THAN OTHERS

Many Christians believe little sins are harmless. Yet so-called "respectable" sins often keep us from fulfilling our responsibility to God and lost men. Respectable sins! Is there such a thing as a "respectable" sin? Don't most of us have a list of sins we think are more heinous than others? My list of real bad "no no's" includes idolatry, hatred, murder, and adultery. But is lying, disobedience, and unbelief less repulsive to God?

Let me suggest three "no no's" on God's list that may not be on ours. On the surface they don't seem important, but they are more important than we realize.

First, the sin of delay or *procrastination*. It was this sin that caused the disciples to miss a great spiritual harvest in the city of Sychar. The Apostle John tells us that he and his fellow disciples went into this small Samaritan city filled with lost people with little thought of witnessing. Jesus does imply His disciples may have considered Sychar a place of possible future harvest. "Do you not say, 'There are yet four months, and then comes the harvest'? Behold, I say to you, lift up your eyes, and look on the fields, that they are white for harvest" (John 4:35).

The disciples put a possible harvest off for a hundred twenty days. But Jesus declares the harvest is so ripe it can't wait until tomorrow. Who is right? What happened that afternoon? "And from that city many of the Samaritans believed in Him because of the word of the woman who testified, 'He told me all the things that I have done' " (John 4:39). For the next two days the harvest continued, "And many more believed because of His word" (4:41).

The average Christian's cardinal sin is a willingness to put things off. The Holy Spirit nudges me to write a letter and my response is, "Yes, of course I will—later." I am under conviction to talk to my neighbor, "Yes, of course I will—later." What about that apology or telephone call I should make. Then there's a check I should write, or gift I should give. What about the time I should set aside for worship, Bible study, and prayer: "Yes, of course I will—later."

Procrastination is born of wilful disobedience, wrong priorities, and spiritual lukewarmness. Is it not true the "saddest words of tongue or pen are 'it might have been' "? Yes, procrastination is ugly sin that often prevents us from pointing a person to Christ.

A high school girl once came to my office crying. After getting hold of herself she told me four of her classmates had just been killed in a terrible automobile accident. I tried to comfort her by

telling her the accident wasn't in any way her
fault.

"But, Mr. Hillis, you don't understand," she
replied. "You see, none of them knew the Lord.
Several times the Lord told me to share my faith
in Jesus with them. I promised I would and fully
intended to. But I always put it off and now it is
too late."

I wept with her. I had too often done the same
thing. She confessed her sin of procrastination
and asked the Lord to teach her to obey Him. He
heard that prayer and today she is a missionary.

Another of these "respectable" sins is indicated
in the story of our Lord with His disciples at
Jacob's well. It is called *discrimination*. It should
never be found in a Christian's heart, but often is.
The soil in which it flourishes is pride! The disciples were victims of this deadly, soul-harming disease. One of the reasons they refused to witness
to the people of Sychar was, "For Jews have no
dealings with Samaritans" (John 4:9). To the disciples, the Samaritans of Sychar were despised
half-breeds, idolaters, and at best, second-class
citizens.

You can see racism and discrimination was not
born in our generation. The prophet Jonah was
God's man but his heart was full of bias and racism. How deep was the race hatred in the heart
of this prophet of God? His one desire was for
tens of thousands of people in the wicked city of
Nineveh to forfeit God's grace and feel His wrath
and punishment.

For eighteen months my family and I lived under the Communist regime in China. I startled myself one day by saying, "I hate Communists." I had watched the Communists destroy the church I had been building for seventeen years. They killed missionaries and imprisoned Chinese Christians. My natural response was to hate.

You see, I was looking at them as Communists, not as "sheep without a shepherd," not as lost souls in desperate need. My attitude was no better than the disciples' with their feeling of hate toward the Samaritans. In hating Communist *ideology,* I was right on. Communist ideology *is* anti-Christ, anti-church, anti-Bible, anti-God, and anti-everything we believe.

But I dare not hate the poor misled lost men and women who are blinded by Communism. Christ died for everyone. The Lord does not see men racially as Japanese, Chinese, Africans, or Latin Americans. Nor does He see them religiously as Muslims, Buddhists, or Daoists; politically as Communists, Republicans, Democrats, Liberals, or Conservatives; or socially as high or low class, educated, uneducated, rich, or poor. Jesus sees men and women as lost sheep. He came "to seek and to save." We need to see men as Jesus saw them. As helpless, hopeless, defenseless sheep needing a shepherd.

There is another reason the disciples missed getting in on the harvest at Sychar. Why did they leave the Lord at Jacob's well and go to the city? They went for a physical reason—they were hungry. They went to buy bread and were *preoccupied* with that task. When they returned and offered the Lord something to eat, He said to them, "My food is to do the will of Him who sent Me, and to accomplish His work" (John 4:34). While His disciples were preoccupied with earthly, physical, material things, Jesus was occupied with spiritual things.

They were not the last ones to fall into the trap of becoming occupied with the temporal and forgetting the eternal. Have you ever put the supermarket ahead of an opportunity to serve Christ?

You recall our Lord's story of a certain rich man. Jesus describes him, "He habitually dressed in purple and fine linen, gaily living in splendor every day" (Luke 16:19). He was wealthy, healthy, and irreligious. He didn't have time for eternal things until it was too late. How easy it is to become preoccupied with making a living, getting ahead, becoming "Mr. Big," building our own kingdoms, and failing to see the hungry souls around us.

Jesus tells another story of a rich man whose land was so productive he said to himself, "What shall I do, since I have no place to store my crops?" After some meditation he said, "This is what I will do: I will tear down my barns and build larger ones, and there I will store all my grain and my goods. And I will say to my soul, 'Soul, you have many goods laid up for many years to come; take your ease, eat, drink and be merry.' " He had it made. Or did he? God said to him, "You fool! This very night your soul is required of you; and now who will own what you have prepared?" (Luke 12:16–20).

Is it possible to overstate the danger of preoccupation? Isn't life more than food and the body more than clothing? We call Him "Lord" but do we serve Him? Do we make the things of His kingdom our priority? He said if we call Him Lord, we will come to Him, hear His words, and act upon them. "Therefore every one who hears these words of Mine, and acts upon them, may be compared to a wise man, who built his house upon the rock; and the rain descended, and the floods came, and the winds blew, and burst against that house; and yet it did not fall; for it had been founded upon the rock" (Matthew 7:24, 25).

How do we deal with the sins of *procrastination, discrimination,* and *preoccupation?* We deal with them by acknowledging His Lordship and seeking first His kingdom (see Matthew 6:33). We must give ourselves to Him in unconditional commitment as Isaac did when he lay on the altar. We should seek *first* the kingdom and glory of God and deny ourselves these so-called "respectable," yet dangerous sins.

CHAPTER 10

◆

WHO KILLED "CONCERN"?

To have a "clean heart" is healthy but to reach the lost, one must have a "concerned heart."

Have you ever wondered what happened to the word *concern?* It may not be considered an old-fashioned word, but it's an old-fashioned idea. Most of us today are too busy to be concerned with anyone but ourselves. We have little or no time to care about the lost and, subconsciously, have put God on our "charity list." This is contrary to our Lord's attitude and those who followed Him. Scripture is filled with evidence of Christ's concern for others:

When Lazarus died, Jesus was *concerned* and gave the dead man life.

When the sinful woman was condemned He was *concerned* and forgave her.

When the temple was dirty He was *concerned* and cleansed it.

When the Pharisees judged and accused He was *concerned* and warned them.

When the unclean lepers cried for healing He was *concerned* and cured them.

When the thief was dying beside Him on the

cross He was *concerned* and took him to heaven with Him.

Christ spelled *CONCERN* with capital letters. The Apostle Paul was so *concerned* for his people that he was willing to take their place in hell if by doing so, Isaac's children could have his place in heaven (see Romans 9:1-3).

Paul's *concern* for the Gentiles was just as deep. The anguish of his cry, "Woe is me if I do not preach the gospel" (1 Corinthians 9:16), reveals the strong pulse of this *concern*.

The first century Church was *concerned* about the lost in Samaria and the hungry in Jerusalem. The Church prayed and sent out anointed witnesses across Asia and Europe. Like her Lord she spelled *CONCERN* with large letters.

The nineteenth century Church was also *concerned* and sent men across every ocean in search of lost multitudes. Hear them:

"Give me Scotland or I die."

"I feel as if I cannot go on living if I cannot reach the millions in the vast inland provinces of China."

These are the heart sounds of men who spelled *CONCERN* with capital letters. By contrast this word is seldom heard and too infrequently practiced today.

In contrast the word "concern" today is too infrequently uttered and seldom practiced. The starving, sick, enslaved, suffering, lost, and dying are everywhere. Their number increases by thirty-four million every year. Is anyone deeply *concerned?* There is little evidence. What happened to the word?

Who put this beautiful word to death? Was she poisoned with the soft drink of selfishness, strangled by the clutching grasp of materialism, smothered by a heavy blanket of indifference? In what coffin did they lay her? Is there hope of her revival?

In answering these questions I condemn myself. Because, I, like you, had a part in her death. We were her pallbearers. But the casket is not yet closed and there is hope of resuscitation. We must pray for "the love of Christ" which flows silently and smoothly like liquid mercury to fill our empty hearts with compassion and *concern*. We desperately need a working compassion that spells *CONCERN* with capital letters.

"If a brother or sister is without clothing and in need of daily food, and one of you says to them, 'Go in peace, be warmed and be filled'; and yet you do not give them what is necessary for their body; what use is that? Even so faith, if it has no works, is dead, being by itself" (James 2:15–17).

We will never find this new compassion if we continue to put our own concerns ahead of God. He must come first in our lives. Our offerings to Him must no longer be "the things we can no longer use." We must give Him the "firstfruit." Most people know this, but forget. I am glad our loving Father knows we need to be prodded. Not long ago He stirred me into action with the return of the robins. The birds returned to Palo Alto on the tail of a flooding rainstorm and looked as soaked and sorry as my soggy front lawn. Deciding they needed some loving encouragement, I started toward the back door with a fresh loaf of bread. Then suddenly an "economic plot" flashed across my mental computer. With bread costing half a dollar a loaf why give them fresh bread? Wouldn't stale bread be good enough? Rummaging around I found just the thing—some pieces so stale they were a little moldy! "If the robins are hungry enough," I reasoned, "they will accept my moldy offering."

I crumbled the stale bread, scattered it on the lawn, and stepped inside to watch through a window. I felt good as I saw the robins cautiously alight on the lawn and ravenously accept my entire offering. Oh, I forgot to tell you, birds are on my charity list!

Feeding the robins triggered a surprising train of thought. I had just offered God's feathered creatures something I couldn't use and didn't want. Was I guilty, consciously or unconsciously, of giving the Creator of those feathered fliers the same kind of offering? The more I pondered the idea the more troubled I became.

As a missionary, I have seen a lot of "moldy bread" given to God. Some of the correspondence in my letter file reeks with mildew. A man once wrote, *"We are getting a new car. We can't get anything for our old one. Could the mission use it? Would it be possible to give me a tax deductible receipt for the blue book price?"*

Was that a "moldy bread" offering? It certainly wasn't "fresh bread." Was the writer's heart motivated by love for God and concern for His creatures or was God simply on his charity list?

Another letter said, *"Our church is sending three boxes of clothes for your missionaries. They are not new, of course, but some of them are quite nice. I am sorry we did not have time to get them cleaned. Our ladies' missionary society is paying the postage so there will be no cost to the mission."* That is *concern* of a kind, but what kind?

In both cases there seemed to be a parallel between the bird offering of "bread I couldn't use." Let me hasten to say we are grateful for every loving gift. What I am talking about are *attitudes* in giving—attitudes of true concern.

And then there was that telephone call. The voice was warm and congenial. *"We are buying a new grand piano,"* she said. *"We have an old upright. It is nearly thirty years old and is still in good condition since no one plays the piano around here too much. I planned to give it to the Goodwill, but my husband thought the mission might want it."*

"Yes," I told her, "the mission would appreciate such a gift."

But as I think back, I wonder if it wasn't "moldy bread" in God's sight. Did they conceive of God as waiting around for a handout?

Do you see what I mean? Have we formed the habit of giving God used objects we no longer need because we've replaced them with something better for ourselves? This certainly is not the way God treats us. Then do I have my priorities in order? What does Jesus say about priorities? "But seek first His kingdom, and His righteousness; and all these things shall be added to you" (Matthew 6:33).

As one studies this verse the word "first" takes on new meaning. God in no way forbids me to provide for my family. On the contrary, the Bible warns, "But if any one does not provide for his own, and especially for those of his household, he . . . is worse than an unbeliever" (1 Timothy 5:8). It is the order of priority that is important. The firstfruit of my talent and toil is to be gladly given to Him. Christ and His cause are to be my "first" concern. Then He promises everything else will fall into proper order and I will lack nothing.

Come to think of it I can't remember ever receiving a letter reading: "We were going to buy a new car (or whatever) *for ourselves, but as we prayed about it the Lord told us to use the money for the extension of His kingdom. Enclosed please find a check. We want the mission to use it to get the message of life to those who are facing death without Christ in Vietnam. It is a joy to do this. We are not worried, for our Heavenly Father has promised to take care of our old car. You see we have claimed the promise, '. . . first His kingdom . . . all these things shall be added . . .' We cannot tell you how very concerned we are for those who are lost.*"

Take special note of the "action" words in our Lord's conversation with the serious rich young man in Matthew 19:21. "*Go . . . sell . . . give . . .* and you *shall have* treasure in heaven." How contrary to one's practice of "hurry . . . purchase

... keep." Here Jesus tells the young man (and us) that what one gives, he keeps, and what one keeps, he loses.

This point becomes crystal clear when I re-study the invitations Jesus gave men to follow Him. When he called Peter and his brother Andrew to "follow," they immediately left their nets, and followed Him (see Matthew 4:19, 20). Later when Jesus asked the brothers, James and John, to give up their fishing business, they did so immediately (see Matthew 4:22). God's plan was more important to these four young men than their own plans and possessions. His *concerns* became their *concerns*.

Notice the difference, however, to the reply of two other young men to the Lord's invitation. "Permit *me first* to go and bury my father," said one. And the second said, "I will follow You, Lord; but *first* permit *me* to say good-bye to those at home" (Luke 9:59, 61). In each case the youth put his personal concern "first." When he finished doing this thing then he would have time to be concerned about God's thing.

Is it not contradictory to call Jesus "Lord," then tell Him we will give Him what He wants only after we have done what we want? Isn't it rather like putting Him on our charity list and saying, "When I have a spare moment I will pray," or, "If I have a spare dollar at the end of this month I will see that you get it"?

Recently a young man told me his goal was to make a million dollars before he was thirty. *He assured me when he reached his goal he hoped to serve God with his time and money.* Was he feeding robins with "moldy bread"? Did he have his priorities right? The answer is no. His first concern was for himself after which he hoped to find time for God.

There was nothing I could do to change this young man, but with thought and honest obedience *I* can change and take God off my charity list and begin seeking *first* His kingdom. I can come to my Father and admit my own self-seeking. I can ask Him to change my attitude. I can stop long enough to ask Him to fill my heart with His *concern* for lost men and women.

CHAPTER 11

◆

THAT HAND ON MY WALLET

How would you react if I ask how much money you have in the bank? In what way would you respond if I continue my prying?

"How much land do you own?

"How much insurance do you carry?

"What do you have in your safety deposit box?

"How much money do you make?

"In what companies do you own shares?

"What do you have in the way of stocks and bonds?

"Do you have a savings account?

"What bank do you use?

"Have you made your will?

"To whom are you giving your money when you die?"

Nobody in his right mind should ask such personal questions. But if I did, you would be on target to conclude me enormously impudent, and ask me to mind my own business.

I said NOBODY! But Jesus doesn't hesitate to meddle. The STARTLING truth is that He feels it's His business to counsel us regarding our personal treasures. Because He is the Source of everything I have, and because He has my personal interest in mind, He clearly explains what I should do and warns me what not to do with my treasures.

Frankly, I think of myself as one of God's "little people." I don't own an oil well, diamond mine, drive a luxury car, or sail an expensive yacht. I own no stocks, bonds, or shares and the local bank owns one-third of my house. As such, I feel little need for financial counsel.

True as this is, Jesus doesn't buy my reasoning. He says everyone has treasures and makes it clear He is not going to check me out on how *much* I have, but on how I invest what I have.

He tells me there are two banks in which I can place my treasures. One on earth and the other in heaven. He carefully explains the returns I will get from each bank. He counsels me not to put my treasures in the Bank of Earth, and gives me sound reasons for it. He advises me to place my treasure in the Bank of Heaven, and makes certain I understand the reason for His advice.

Yet this is as far as He goes, because like a good financial counselor, He gives me full responsibility for handling my treasures. However, the weight of this responsibility and the knowledge that I will be held accountable cause me to carefully study His investment plan.

His first instruction is to leave the Bank of Earth alone. Immediately I am faced with a difficulty because this bank is conveniently equipped with a drive-up window. Furthermore, it's the bank most of my friends patronize and promises six per cent interest on my investment. But Jesus warns about placing my treasure there: "Do not lay up for yourselves treasures upon earth, where moth and rust destroy, and where thieves break in and steal" (Matthew 6:19).

And who has not seen what moth and rust can do? A family of moths can reduce a beautiful expensive garment to a see-through rag. Noiseless, unending, corroding rust turns handsome useful automobiles into useless ugly eyesores. Rust can transform a mighty ocean vessel into an unseaworthy floating coffin. The thieves of inflation, embezzlement, mismanagement, high taxes, and bankruptcy can absorb and wipe out one's treasure.

Our former Overseas Crusades headquarters' office illustrates this. An owner of the Roma Wines distillery once proudly displayed it as his palace. It was, afterall, located on an important Los Angeles street and received some of the city's most beautiful and important people. But its days of glory were now past. The treasured temple had become a "termite terrace." Soon after our mission moved to Palo Alto a wrecking crew moved in with their great swinging steel ball and in forty-eight hours the cement, steel, and wood *treasure* was a pile of trash. There is something sad and meaningless about investing one's treasure in the Bank of Earth. It is so temporary and easily consumed by weather and worm.

Jesus warns about another frightening effect of putting my treasure in the Bank of Earth, "For where your treasure is, there will your heart be also" (Matthew 6:21). If my savings account is on earth my thinking, planning, emotions, and heart will also be on earth.

The treasure I give to God is an "unfailing treasure." It can't be touched. It makes me "rich toward God" (Luke 12:21). The very giving of a treasure to God weans my heart from the world and makes me *"think heaven"* (Luke 12:34). Because my treasure is in heaven my thoughts are aimed differently and eternity becomes far more important than the present.

This doesn't mean one should rush out and sell everything he owns. No, our Lord is talking about priorities. When He says, "Seek *first,*" He clearly implies there is a "second." I am to be a wise businessman, farmer, or whatever. I am to pay my debts and provide for my family. But God is not to be on my charity list—His kingdom is to come *first.*

It is little wonder the beloved Apostle John did not place a period at the close of his admonition, "Do not love the world," but hastened to add, "nor the things in the world" (1 John 2:15). The world is the body of the octopus but "the things" are the long strong tentacles that bleed our spiritual life and drain our desire for heaven.

I must serve God or money. I cannot serve both. But if I make Jesus my Master I can make riches (my treasure) serve God. Therefore, Jesus commands, ". . . Lay up for yourselves treasures in *heaven*" (Matthew 6:20). I listen to His command. I recognize it is reasonable and so I obey. In a planned, practical way I use the treasure He gives me to extend His kingdom. I do my giving while I am living. There are many opportunities to invest in heaven, and I pray that God will make me a wise steward.

And God will give wisdom. Part of my treasure is destined for the local Body of Christ . . . part is used to build a hospital in an undeveloped area . . . to send a missionary abroad . . . to support a Gospel broadcast in the Orient . . . to help a citywide crusade in Latin America . . . to print a Bible correspondence course in a strange African language—my treasure is stored in heaven. There it's out of the ravenous appetite of moth, rust, wealth, worms, and thieves. There, gains are high and dividends eternal. The President of the Bank of Heaven promises ten thousand per cent interest (one hundredfold—Matthew 19:29). He is Savior and doesn't play with figures. He will keep His promise. In what other bank can I be sure of such profit?

The wisest thing you and I can do today is to inventory our treasures and immediately switch as much as possible from the Bank of Earth to the Bank of Heaven. Let's make sure there is a nail-pierced hand on our wallets. Only then can we prove our love for the Savior and concern for the lost.

CHAPTER 12

◆

MY ACHING KNEES!

My kneecap is more important than my wallet. Prayer invests the common man with a kind of omnipotence and places God's greatest weapon in his hands. Though you and I are pitifully weak, yet we hold a strategic role in the spiritual warfare against Satan. When we pray, souls bound in sin are freed. Only our lack of belief can shackle omnipotence because faith releases God's power. The simple prayer of faith is more powerful than many armies.

For our missionary friend out in the heat of spiritual battle, prayer is his greatest need. It makes the difference between victory and defeat. I marvel that light travels around the world seven times every second. But the result of prayer can be felt in any corner of the earth the instant it is uttered. Prayer is our invisible, irresistible weapon. Only in answer to prayer can the powers of darkness be driven back and spiritual prisoners held by satanic superstition set free. It is my purpose to show how easily you can become proficient in the use of this mightiest of all weapons.

One of the important Biblical expressions for bringing lost men to Christ is "gathering the harvest." Harvesting is seasonal, and the season for this harvest reoccurs with each generation. Since the death and resurrection of Christ, there have been no less than *sixty* harvest seasons. The command of the Lord of the harvest is that the Gospel should be preached to every person in every nation in every generation. It is clear from Scripture that God desires a harvest to be gathered in each generation. It follows then, in order to gather this harvest, God needs harvesters. Christ Himself said, "The harvest is plentiful, but the laborers are few; therefore beseech the Lord of the harvest to send out laborers into His harvest" (Luke 10:2).

These "farm hands" are not all to come from America. Wherever there are Christians there are potential harvesters. This makes it imperative that we pray for the Lord of the harvest to send forth national laborers as well as American missionaries. In our praying we dare not get caught in the trap of provincialism. God expects the Church world-wide to help gather the world-wide harvest. Provincialism is a form of spiritual nearsightedness. Men gifted in the use of the spiritual sickle are to go forth *from* every tribe and tongue *to* every tribe and tongue. So first of all we pray for harvesters.

We are not only to pray because God ordered it. We must pray because intercession brings to the battlefield the irresistible power of God. Satan is called "the god of this world." He not only holds man captive but has "blinded the minds of them that believe not." Mankind walks in darkness, lives in fear and is held in bondage. If man is to be set free, Satan must be pushed back, the chains of superstition broken and blinded eyes opened. This can be done only through the preaching of the Gospel and by the power of God to answer prayer.

In Scripture there are a number of illustrations proving that the difference between victory and defeat is prayer or lack of it. Let me refer to just one. The Amalekites vowed they would destroy Israel and arrayed themselves in battle. "So Moses said to Joshua, 'Choose men for us, and go out, fight against Amalek. Tomorrow I will station myself on the top of the hill with the staff of God in my hand.' And Joshua did as Moses told him, and fought against Amalek; and Moses, Aaron, and Hur went up to the top of the hill. So it came about when Moses held his hand up, that Israel prevailed, and when he let his hand down, Amalek prevailed. But Moses' hands were heavy. Then they took a stone and put it under him, and he sat on it; and Aaron and Hur supported his hands, one on one side and one on the other. Thus his hands were steady until the sun set. So Joshua overwhelmed Amalek and his people with the edge of the sword" (Exodus 17:9–13).

The difference between victory and defeat was not the prowess of the men of Israel or the strategy of their commander-in-chief. The difference was prayer.

Today God is still selecting men, some to go to far-flung spiritual battlefields and others to stay on the top of the hill in prayer. "You did not choose Me, but I chose you, and appointed you, that you should go and bear fruit, and that your fruit should remain; that whatever you ask of the Father in My name, He may give it to you" (John 15:16).

I want you to know that more prayer means more victories. I also want you to know that we in America can pray to God in heaven for a missionary in Brazil and change fruit*less*ness to fruit*ful*ness.

When should we pray for missions and missionaries? The Bible gives several time guides for prayer. There are Biblical records of extended times in prayer. Moses prayed for forty days and forty nights. Nehemiah, hearing of the sad condition of Jerusalem, prayed over a period of four months. So concerned and intense was his prayer, that it showed on his face. On more than one occasion Jesus prayed all night.

Such extended prayer was due to a special burden or problem. The intercessor was saying to God, as Jacob did, "I will not let you go unless you bless me" (Genesis 32:26). Such prayer may happen once or several special times in a lifetime. It is not a daily pattern.

Speaking of patterns, David had one worth following. He said, "Evening and morning and at noon, I will complain and murmur, And He will hear my voice" (Psalm 55:17). Apparently Daniel practiced the same prayer schedule, ". . . and he continued kneeling on his knees three times a day, praying and giving thanks before his God, as he had been doing previously" (Daniel 6:10). In every Christian's life there should be a planned prayer time each day. A prayer list and a prayer map will make the time more effective.

The Apostle Paul says, "With all prayer and petition pray at all times in the Spirit, and with this in view, be on the alert with all perseverance and petition for all the saints" (Ephesians 6:18). No witness for Christ was ever busier than Paul. He was an author, preacher, teacher, traveler, and missionary. Yet *he* found time to pray and to pray for all saints. How is this possible?

Paul had learned to "pray by means of the Spirit." With him it was "praying without ceasing." Though he no doubt had set times for intercession, he had learned to pray in all places at all times. Writing to the little group of believers in the powerful, political city of Rome, he said, "For God, whom I serve in my spirit in the preaching of the gospel of His Son, is my witness as to how unceasingly I make mention of you" (Romans 1:9). To the believers in the carnal, cultural center at Corinth, he said, "I thank my God always concerning you, for the grace of God which was given you in Christ Jesus" (1 Corinthians 1:4). To the church in the idolatrous city of Ephesus, he wrote, "do not cease giving thanks for you, while making mention of you in my prayers" (Ephesians 1:16).

To the Christians of Philippi, Paul gave this assurance, "I thank my God in all my remembrance of you" (Philippians 1:3). For the believers of Colosse, whom he had perhaps never seen, Paul had this word, "We give thanks to God, the

Father of our Lord Jesus Christ, praying always for you" (Colossians 1:3). Thinking back on his short but fruitful time in Thessalonica, the apostle wrote to that dynamic church, "We give thanks to God always for all of you, making mention of you in our prayers; constantly bearing in mind your work of faith and labor of love and steadfastness of hope in our Lord Jesus Christ in the presence of our God and Father (1 Thessalonians 1:2, 3).

We often think we are too busy to pray, or if we do pray we pray only for our own little group. Paul's intercession circled Asia and Europe and included groups and individuals. Writing to Timothy, he says, "I thank God, whom I serve with a clear conscience the way my forefathers did, as I constantly remember you in my prayers night and day" (2 Timothy 1:3).

If you take time to read Ephesians 1:17–20, you will notice Paul does not pray in vague generalities. Rather his prayer is focused because he knew generalities are ineffective. Focused prayer is a fighting force.

Since we now know we must pray, it's up to us as individuals to make the time for prayer. One remaining question is, "How shall I pray for missionaries and for what should I pray?"

We already know we are to "pray the Lord of the harvest to send forth laborers." But how are we to pray for that laborer after God has heard prayer and sent him forth? First, pray that he will have vision to see the harvest. It is entirely possible for a missionary to fail to see prepared hearts, even though he stands in their midst. This should not overly surprise you because Christ's own disciples were caught in the same position.

In a previous chapter we saw Jesus sending his disciples into the city of Sychar on a routine task to buy bread. There was a host of prepared hearts in that city, but not one of the disciples thought of presenting the Savior to them. When the disciples returned to the well where Jesus was sitting, He said to them, "Do not say, 'There are yet four months, and then comes the harvest'? Behold, I say to you, lift up your eyes, and look on the fields, that they are white for harvest" (John 4:35).

The harvester not only needs vision but he must have skill in handling the spiritual sickle. It is his task to deal with the wicked woman of John 4, or the highly moral, religious Nicodemus of John 3. He must be prepared to wisely touch every stratum of life. He must be able to deal with the atheist who says there is no God, or with the Hindu who claims there are three hundred million gods.

The spiritual harvester must have a willing spirit and dare not be lazy. In the Orient the farmer is the first one up in the morning. What time does the missionary get up?

You may know one of God's harvesters living in a hot, humid tropical country. From his letters you learn the people with whom he works have a simple philosophy of life, expressed in the one word—"tomorrow." Why should they be in a hurry? Shoes and clothes are not needed. Food, yes.

But that is easily gathered from the rich jungles. Are you aware that a hot climate and a lazy people can make a zealous harvester an indifferent laborer?

On the North American continent our great wheat fields are harvested by mighty combines. The sickle is the only tool of millions of farmers in other parts of the world. Theirs is a back-breaking job. From sunup to sundown, up one row and down the other, men swing the sickle, gathering in every stock of grain. This requires not only a willing spirit but a strong back and a good physique. If the missionary is to keep pace and gather the harvest, he also must have health and strength. There are far too many physical casualties on foreign lands. Satan uses disease and accidents to make God's servants retreat from the field of battle.

Take the tests and temptations that come your way. Multiply them a hundred times and you understand something of what the missionary faces. He is both a laborer and a soldier. His battle is physical and spiritual. His enemies are disease, darkness, dangers, death, and demons. He must have protection, provision, wisdom, vision, zeal, and power. All these can be his in answer to our prayers.

If you and I care about men who are lost we should faithfully intercede by name for those who are in distant lands seeking to reach the lost.

WHAT UNLIMITED OPPORTUNTIES!!
GET INVOLVED WITH MISSIONS
WRITE
READ
GIVE
PRAY

CHAPTER 13

◆

JUMP IN—OR COP OUT!

As Christians we face a grave responsibility. Men are in darkness and we have the LIGHT. Men are starving and we have the "Bread of life." Men are afflicted with the soul-destroying disease of sin and in Christ we have the cure. Our obligation to lost men is frightening—almost overwhelming.

"When I say to the wicked, 'You shall surely die'; and you do not warn him or speak out to warn the wicked from his wicked way that he may live, that wicked man shall die in his iniquity, but his blood I will require at your hand" (Ezekiel 3:18).

What does this verse mean? Is it not saying that if we are indifferent and careless about a lost world God will hold us guilty?

Yes, I quoted from the Old Testament, but Paul brings out the same truth in the New Testament: "And when they resisted and blasphemed, he shook out his garments and said to them, 'Your blood be upon your own heads, I am clean; from now on I shall go to the Gentiles'" (Acts 18:6). Only after the apostle gave men a clear chance

to hear and reject the Gospel did he have peace
... the peace of a debt paid to God and lost men.

Jesus said, "If you keep My commandments,
you will abide in My love; just as I have kept My
Father's commandments, and abide in His love"
(John 15:10). Will our personal devotion to Christ
motivate us to do something about His command
to carry the Gospel to every creature? If the evan-
gelization of every man lies nearest to the heart
of the Savior, should it not have priority in our
lives? In a real way, the measure of our zeal for
missions is the measure of our devotion to Christ.
Knowing this, we ask, "What can I do?" Here are
some answers.

We can witness. Faced with a world that has
more winnable people than ever before, we don't
dare be silent, indifferent Christians. We must
not count the cost. We must pay the price, obey
the command, and by all means get the Good
News to all men.

The New Testament makes it all so transpar-
ent: "... and he who sows bountifully shall also
reap bountifully" (2 Corinthians 9:6).

Today 10,000 persons will die from malnutri-
tion and 124,000 from other causes. Today 324,-
000 babies will be born and the net gain will be
190,000 persons ...

> ... 190,000 more mouths to feed
>
> ... 190,000 more bodies to clothe
>
> ... 190,000 more minds to educate
>
> ... 190,000 more souls to be reached for Jesus
>   Christ.

It is plain to see the Church's task (your's and mine) is a growing one ... by 190,000 a day.

On the Mount of Olives our Lord clearly spelled out the work He expects us to do. "You must witness to your world," He said (see Acts 1:8).

Our witness must be "in depth," including the poor, rich, educated, uneducated, the laboring man, business executive, child, housewife, youth, aged, religious, and nonreligious.

Our witness must be "in breadth." Touching those who can be touched in personal daily contact. Reaching out by prayer, letter, telephone, radio, television, and by our missionary partners to the outer fringes of geography where unreached souls silently wait the awesome experience of death, having never heard of Jesus Christ, the Giver of life.

We can tell our immediate world (family, relatives, neighbors, business associates, friends) in our own home-spun vocabulary how Jesus saved us and how He longs to redeem them.

We can read good books on witnessing and missions. Then we can share those books with others. Many Christian homes have no up-to-date missionary books. Change that situation in your home.

We can teach our children about missons and the great need for missionaries. Read them the stories of missionaries in the book of Acts and of great missionaries who have carried on in the last two thousand years. This can be done in a home situation or Sunday school class. In any case, missions must begin with the beginners both at home and in church.

The many lethal problems and temptations missionaries face such as mental and spiritual darkness, discouragement, disease, daily physical dangers, and demonic powers, should be singled out in your prayers.

Start a missionary prayer cell in your home, church, school, or office. A few years ago five young men started such a cell in Southern California. They met every Tuesday morning at five to pray around the world. In six years all of them were in full-time service. Four of them went to foreign lands.

Back your church's missionary program. Help the missionary committee put together an annual missionary conference if your church does not already have one.

We can give. Of the Christians of Macedonia, Paul wrote, "For I testify that according to their ability, and beyond their ability they gave of their own accord" (2 Corinthians 8:3). What one can afford is the "tithe and offering." What one cannot afford he gives beyond the tithe and offering *"by faith."* He believes God will make him a channel of support beyond what he has. Dr. Oswald Smith called this kind of giving "faith promise." Hundreds of churches and thousands of Christians have proved it works. Anything can happen when you begin trusting God!

A few years ago it was my privilege to speak at a small missionary conference in Indiana. Eleven families met in a rented hall as they had no church building. But they did have a burning zeal for missions and all of them were involved in faith promises. Today they have four hundred members, a church that stands to the glory of God and yearly faith promises to foreign missions of more than six figures.

And there is something else you can do. Missionaries are often sent to lonely places. They need to hear from you, and know about you, your family, the church, and their friends. "Like cold water to a weary soul, So is good news from a distant land" (Proverbs 25:25). Include a picture now and then.

My first term in China was a long and lonely eight years with too few letters. After I returned I spoke at a church in Oregon and told them about my work. At the close of the service, a friend said, "I want you to know that although I did not write I did pray for you every day for eight years."

I wanted to say, "Oh why didn't you write and tell me? I so needed the encouragement your letters could have given." And what did I want to hear? Everything! News of weddings and weather, babies and banquets, comings and goings, peoples and programs—everything you were experiencing. Not reams of Scripture. I have a Bible and I read it. Your letter can refresh and encourage but only if you write it.

I have another idea. Why not adopt a missionary? Make yourself aware of his needs and help provide them. Get so close that he will share his victories and acknowledge his defeats. When he hurts—you hurt. When he laughs—you laugh. Make him a part of your life and family, so that his work is your work and his concern is your concern.

If you do the Lord of the harvest may show you other ways to get involved which might include preparing for foreign missionary service. In any case, do something. Don't cop out. Put your life potential into the hand of your omnipotent Father and in His strength get with it. He has commanded us to care. We *are* our "brother's keeper!"

CHAPTER 14

◆

"HOW DO I FIT IN?"

In a previous chapter I listed a number of needs for those who are committed to a foreign assignment for God. But what are the things that help qualify a person for cross-cultural service?

A hundred and fifty years ago, the wife of Adoniram Judson (pioneer missionary to Burma) wrote: "In encouraging young men to come as missionaries, do use the greatest caution. One strong, brash-headed, conscientiously obstinate man can ruin us. Humble, quiet, persevering men . . . men of sound sterling talents, of decent accomplishments, and some natural aptitude to acquire a language . . . men of amiable, yielding temper, willing to take the lowest place, to be least and a servant of all . . . men who enjoy much closet religion, who live near God, and are willing to suffer all things for Christ's sake without being proud of it."

This letter is one hundred fifty years old and the English the author uses is old. But the list she gives is as up-to-date as tomorrow. God needs a man, ten thousand men, but not just any kind. God needs special men.

It should go without saying that God needs

men with a "born again" experience. Because only as one has had a personal life-changing encounter with Jesus Christ can he introduce others to the Savior. The first missionary couple of a large denomination to arrive in Taiwan were delightful born-again people. God blessed their ministry and soon they found it necessary to call for help. A cable to their mission authorities in the United States said, "God is blessing. Church growing, Need assistance. Please send born-again missionary couple. Urgent."

Eleven months later the requested couple arrived. They possessed the academic training needed and were healthy and dedicated. But neither was saved. How do I know? Easy! Both of them accepted Christ during their time in Chinese language school. In this case it turned out all right, though it seems a bit far out to send representatives of Christ to foreign lands who don't really know the One they are sent to represent.

God needs men with a solid, practical faith and confidence in the whole Word of God. Do you really know the Bible? Are you free from doctrinal hobbies? Too often I have seen national Christians confused by missionaries who insisted their interpretation of some doctrinal point was the only right one.

I know a middle-aged missionary who should still be on the field, but is not. The national Church requested his mission to send him home. Why?

"He makes us feel inferior. He insists he is always right and never wrong. He declares the

Holy Spirit is his teacher and infers *he,* not the Holy Spirit, is our teacher."

I am sure the missionary didn't want to make that kind of impression, but he did. As a result, he is no longer serving in the Orient.

In Part II of this book our word was *"concern."* It is now fair to ask, do you have a *concerned* compassionate love for the lost? If so, God can use you. If not, He can't. Through His servant, Paul, He said, "If I speak with the tongues of men and of angels, but do not have love, I have become a noisy gong or a clanging cymbal. And if I have the gift of prophecy, and know all mysteries and all knowledge; and if I have all faith, so as to remove mountains, but do not have love, I am nothing. And if I give all my possessions to feed the poor, and if I deliver my body to be burned, but do not have love, it profits me nothing" (1 Corinthians 13:1–3).

Love—or nothing. It was love that motivated Christ. "And seeing the multitudes, He felt compassion for them, because they were distressed and downcast like sheep without a shepherd" (Matthew 9:36). What animal is more defenseless than a sheep? It is no coincidence that Christ likens men to sheep. Man is terribly helpless against Satan the roaring lion, the subtle serpent; Satan the deceiving angel of light.

The Apostle Paul knew and felt man's helplessness in the face of this evil foe and from a heart full of love for the lost he cried, ". . . woe is me if I do not preach the gospel" (1 Corinthians 9:16). Paul also gives us the source of his compassion when he says, "For the love of Christ controls us ..." (2 Corinthians 5:14). God's missionary must be filled with God's love. A man without compassion is as worthless as a car without gas or a plane without wings.

God is looking for a man with a proven ministry who has demonstrated that the "Gospel is the power of God" in his own life, and through his testimony has demonstrated that "it is the power of God" in someone else's life. God needs a man who has demonstrated his ability to lovingly handle the deep spiritual problems of the Body of Christ.

God is looking for one who is not afraid of Satan, who will not barter the will of God for a softer, safer place; one who is spiritually mature. With maturity there is sometimes rigidity, but one must be willing to adjust to those to whom he goes. He dare not have the "play-my-way-or-I-will-take-my-marbles-and-go-home" attitude. He must recognize that those with whom he works may be different but this does not necessarily make them wrong. He must make the nationals' life his textbook. He must master their language, mimic their customs, and follow their good habits.

Most Americans are not known for their humility and as such have been nicknamed "Ugly" by many outside the U.S. No missionary, however, should ever be known for an abrasive, pretentious attitude. And although God is looking for leaders, He wants men who lead by example, not command. Missionaries should go to minister rather than to be ministered unto, and should be prepared to serve under nationals. God wants men willing to wear the towel and wash the national brothers' feet ... men with faith and confidence in God, not in themselves. God wants men who when they preach, believe there will be a harvest, and when they teach, expect to see changed lives. God needs men who have confidence in the work of the Holy Spirit and believe the Spirit of God can and will do anything in the life of a national that He has already done in their own lives.

One of the humblest servants of God I ever knew was not American but Chinese. For thirty years he walked the muddy roads of inland China preaching the Gospel and teaching the Christians. He asked nothing for his service. He had little education but a great love for God and His Word. Thousands across China found Christ through his life and ministry. He was humble as a servant should be. God uses humble men.

In almost every land today there is a Christian church with a need for teachers. And there are at least two types of teachers needed. The first comes from behind the pulpit or desk and takes place in church, school, Bible school, or seminary. Then there are teachers who teach by example. Jesus used both methods. He is the One who said, "Follow Me, and I will make you fishers of men" (Matthew 4:19). The national Christian will accompany you but will not go if all you do is preach *at* him.

I think of the many sermons I gave in China on

"Go into all the world and preach the gospel to all creation" (Mark 16:15). I longed for every Christian to become a witness, but nothing happened until the day I said, "Instead of preaching and telling you to go, *I* will go. Will you follow me?" They did, and people were saved, churches were born, and a harvest was gathered. God is looking for men who are prepared to lead by example.

This was the Apostle Paul's method. To the Thessalonians he wrote, "You also became imitators of us and of the Lord ..." (1 Thessalonians 1:6). To the Corinthians he said, "Be imitators of me, just as I also am of Christ" (1 Corinthians 11:1). Paul taught his followers to be witnesses through lip and life. In a previous chapter I mentioned the great need for prayer. God is looking for men of prayer who will go to foreign lands. Unfortunately prayer is a missing ingredient in many lives. Men do not know how to pray. But without prayer the foreign missionary is lost. Why? Because he is engaged in spiritual warfare. He is called upon to cross enemy lines, search out the captives of Satan, break the chains, and set men free. His spiritual weapons are "the sword of the Spirit and the shield of faith."

"Ask, and you will receive" (John 16:24) becomes the missionary's hallmark of confidence. If you want to be a missionary it must be your hallmark.

Some of the men Jesus chose were ignorant, uneducated men, others highly educated. There is both the Peter and the Paul. In many lands today the nationals themselves have high standards of education. Therefore, it is not surprising they demand the same in a missionary. God does not want the "short-cut Charlie." He is not looking for a man so anxious to get to the field that he drops out of school. God is looking for a man who begins and finishes a task before he takes his next step. He is also looking for a man with twenty-twenty vision and a wide-angle lens: one who sees the whole world and loves the "whole Body of Christ." God is looking for a man to whom color, geography, denomination, and all other considerations are secondary to the cause of Christ in the world.

If you are this kind of man or are willing to become such a man, God has a place for you in reaching the lost.

No matter the logic
or arguments
of men—

"Let God be true."

And may your response and mine be that of the great Apostle Paul, "For I believe God, that it will turn out exactly as I have been told."